DOCUMENTATION STANDARDS FOR COMPUTER SYSTEMS

SECOND EDITION

To Aina and Ivar

Documentation Standards for Computer Systems

Second Edition

Norman L. Enger, PhD, CDP
President
Applied Management Systems
Bethesda, Maryland

THE
TECHNOLOGY
PRESS
Incorporated

Library of Congress Cataloging in Publication Data

Enger, Norman L
Documentation standards for computer systems.

Bibliography: p.
Includes index.
1. Electronic data processing documentation.
I. Title.
QA76.9.D6E53 1980 001.6'42 79-5289
ISBN 0-89321-119-2

Published by:
The Technology Press, Incorporated
Box 125
Fairfax Station, Virginia 22039

Manufactured in the United States of America

9 8 7 6 5 4 3 2 1 80 81 82 83 84

PREFACE

The original edition of **Documentation Standards for Computer Systems** was published in 1976. Since that time, I have visited with many industrial, commercial, and academic organizations that have successfully adopted these standards

Inasmuch as the book continues to be in public demand in this country and others, the publisher recommended that a second edition be made available. Therefore, I have revised and expanded the material presented in the first edition. The intended audience for the first edition was the seasoned computer professional. Now, the narrative sections of this new edition will be useful not only to computer professionals, but to students and to novices in the computer industry.

Each of the chapters in the second edition includes revised and expanded material. The system's life cycle of a computer application and the sixteen key life cycle documents are explained more fully. Where appropriate, the discussions include new analysis, design, and programming techniques that affect the system's life cycle and its products. The original Preface has been retained because it is still timely with regard to the objectives of the book and the importance of management's commitment to documentation.

I would like to thank my colleagues in the computer industry who participated in the research for this new edition.

N. L. E.

PREFACE FROM THE FIRST EDITION

This documentation standards manual was developed by the management consulting company Applied Management Systems, Inc. under contract to the Commonwealth of Virginia and several other governmental and industrial clients. The Directorate of Automation, Policy, Technology, and Standards in the U.S. Department of Defense has formulated a number of excellent guidelines and procedures for the development of automated data systems that were utilized as the foundation for this manual.

The manual outlines and discusses the contents of sixteen key documents that normally would be produced during the design and implementation of a computer application. A systems analyst or programmer can use this manual as a primer that describes the contents of key documents necessary for the documentation of a computer system.

The amount and quality of documentation produced during the development of a computer application will vary with the seriousness of management's commitment to documentation, the magnitude of the project, the project organization structure, and the technical environment in which the application is being developed.

The challenge to management is to determine the amount of documentation necessary for specific types of projects, to balance the need for documentation with the need for the production of operational computer applications, and to enforce the documentation standards that have been adopted by the organization.

Most analysts and programmers look askance at rules for documentation. However, good documentation is necessary if management is to control and be responsible for the accuracy and responsiveness of computer programs and systems.

N.L.E.

CONTENTS

ILLUSTRATIONS

NUMBER TITLE AND PAGE

1. INTRODUCTION

As a safeguard of an organization's resources, documentation of a computer application is as important as accounting practices. The usefulness of proper documents as safeguards is in their comprehensibility to others besides their authors. Comprehensible documents, the result of technical writing skills and sufficient time for preparation, reflect good management.

A distinct set of documents about tasks and responsibilities is associated with each step as a computer application evolves through a life cycle. This life cycle includes a specific series of steps, from the initiation of a computer application to its final live operation. This chapter presents an overview of the documentation recommended for the various stages of the system's life cycle. Documentation requirements will vary from organization to organization and, therefore, management can expect that these guidelines need customizing.

OBJECTIVE OF STANDARDS

With documentation standards incorporated when work on designing a software system is recorded, documentation serves to:

- Provide managers in the user organization with documents for review to verify at significant developmental milestones (review points) that requirements have been met and that resources should continue to be expended.

- Record technical information to allow coordinating later development and user modification of the system.

- Ensure that authors of documents and managers of project development have a guide to follow in preparing and checking documentation.

- Provide guidelines to ensure uniformity of format and content of the system's documentation.

- Reduce the disruptive effects of personnel turnover.

- Establish criteria of performance for project managers and system personnel.

The project manager should verify that the documentation requirements for a particular project are understood. A documentation plan should be established early in the process of project development and include the types to be produced, the dates that these documents must be available, and quality assurance procedures. Project documentation should be reviewed periodically to ensure that it is being prepared in a timely and proper manner.

The authors of documents should be certain that they have a basic understanding of the requirements stated in this book and an understanding of writing for the audience who will use their documents.

When object documents describing a system have been prepared, they must be reviewed to ensure their adequacy, completeness, and adherence to the applicable standards. Pertinent comments should be returned to the originators of the documents. System documentation should be maintained and updated as changes to the system are implemented.

STEPS IN SYSTEM DEVELOPMENT

System development, or the development of a computer application, requires a specific sequence of steps. The six basic steps comprising the system's life cycle are: **initiation, analysis, design, development, implementation,** and **operation.** These steps are shown in Illustration **1-1** and are discussed individually in Chapters Two through Seven.

TYPES OF DOCUMENTS

A number of different documents will be produced in the development of an automated data system. Inasmuch as each document will be written for a specific audience, the documents will differ greatly in tone and structure. Illustration **1-2** relates these documents to the six steps in the system's life cycle.

FUNCTIONS AND PRODUCTS OF SYSTEM'S LIFE CYCLE

STEPS IN LIFE CYCLE	PRIMARY FUNCTION	PRODUCTION OF DOCUMENTS
INITIATION	START PROJECT	• User Request • Proposal and Estimate of Cost • Feasibility Study • Project Plan
ANALYSIS	ANALYZE REQUIREMENTS	• Functional Description • Data Requirements Document
DESIGN	DESIGN NEW SYSTEM	• System/Subsystem Specifications • Data Base Specifications • Program Specifications
DEVELOPMENT	DEVELOP SOFTWARE	• Program Documentation
IMPLEMENTATION	INSTALL NEW SYSTEM	• Test Plan • Test Analysis Report • User's Manual
OPERATION	OPERATE NEW SYSTEM	• Operations Manual • Maintenance Manual • Evaluation Report

Illustration 1-1.

DOCUMENTS PRODUCED DURING SYSTEM'S LIFE CYCLE

INITIATION	ANALYSIS	DESIGN	DEVELOPMENT	IMPLEMENTATION	OPERATION
• Initiation	• Definition	• Detailed Design	• Programming	• Testing • Conversion	• Operation • Maintenance
• User Request	• Functional Description	• System/ Subsystem Specifications	• Program Documentation	• Test Plan	• Operations Manual
• Proposal and Estimate of Cost	• Data Requirements Document	• Data Base Specifications		• Test Analysis Report	• Maintenance Manual
• Feasibility Study		• Program Specifications		• User's Manual	• Evaluation Report
• Project Plan					

Illustration 1-2.

Sixteen documents that may be produced during the development of a computer application are listed and defined as follows:

- The **User Request** is the user document requesting data processing services. This document would be written in general terms to describe a desired computer application.

- The **Proposal and Estimate of Cost** is the document from the Data Center or contractor prepared to satisfy the User Request.

- The **Feasibility Study** is undertaken to determine if the benefits to be derived from a proposed new system justify the development time and cost.

- The **Project Plan** defines the tasks comprising a project, makes personnel assignments, assigns time schedules, establishes developmental milestones, and estimates development costs.

- The **Functional Description** is the result of system analysis. This technical document, written in language for the user, defines the system to be developed. The user should review this document and request changes prior to detailed system development.

- A **Data Requirements Document** may be developed to list and define data elements which the system must handle and to communicate data collection requirements to the user.

- The **System/Subsystem Specifications** define the logical components of the system to be developed.

- The **Data Base Specifications** define the structure, contents, and operational characteristics of the system's data base.

- The **Program Specifications** define the requirements and characteristics of each program to be developed.

- The **Program Documentation** consists of the logic flowcharts and narrative descriptions supporting each program that has been developed.

- The **Test Plan** specifies the sequence of steps and materials necessary to test the system prior to live operation.

- The **Test Analysis Report** specifies the condition of the system and programs after testing.

- The **User's Manual** describes the system to the user. The manual shows how to provide input to the system and how to interpret output from the system.

- The **Operations Manual** contains the information and operating procedures necessary to operate the system that has been developed. It is directed toward the computer operations staff that will actually run the system.

- The **Maintenance Manual** contains specific information on each computer program. Its purpose is to permit the maintenance of the system in terms of changes.

- The **Evaluation Report** is prepared after a system becomes operational and indicates whether the operational system is meeting design specifications.

DOCUMENTATION

Documentation is the record of system development. It is the primary source of reference for system review or modification. Illustration **1-3** shows the relationship between types of documents and various project documentation folders.

Documentation can be classified into either of the following categories:

Project Control Documentation

Project control documentation provides information on the progress of a project and on the utilization of manpower, time, and machine resources. The **Project Plan** is the primary reference point for this project control documentation.

Project Documentation

Project documentation consists of the correspondence, charts, specifications, manuals, and other materials created as a result of the work completed to comply with a User Request for service. The logical components of project documentation created during system development are **Project**, **System**, **Program**, **Production**, and **User Folders**. The **Project Folder** would usually be maintained in the office of the Director of Data Processing. The **System**, **Program**, and **Production Folders** would normally reside in a central Documentation Library with controlled circulation procedures. The **User Folder** would be located in the office of the user.

FOLDERS FOR PROJECT DOCUMENTATION

PROJECT FOLDER

- Correspondence
- User Request
- Proposal and Estimate of Cost
- Project Plan

SYSTEM FOLDER

- Feasibility Study
- Functional Description
- Data Requirements Document
- System Design Report
    - System/Subsystem Specifications
    - Data Base Specifications
    - Program Specifications
    - Test Plan
    - User's Manual
- Evaluation Report

PROGRAM FOLDER

- Program Documentation
- Test Analysis Report

PRODUCTION FOLDER

- Operations Manual
- Maintenance Manual

USER FOLDER

- User's Manual

ILLUSTRATION 1-3.

The various project documentation folders and their contents are described as follows:

• The **Project Folder**, in historical sequence, contains a record of user correspondence and management information related to a project.

• The **System Folder** contains records of the system analysis and design work completed during the project. For example, copies of the Functional Description and the System Design Report would be contained in this folder. The latter includes the System/Subsystem Specifications, Data Base Specifications, Program Specifications, Test Plan, and User's Manual. A copy of the Evaluation Report comparing live system operation to design specifications would also be contained in the folder.

• The **Program Folder** contains the Program Documentation of the system and a copy of the Test Analysis Report. It also contains block diagrams, program listings, program test results, and similar information necessary to understand and maintain computer programs.

• The **Production Folder** contains the Operations Manual and the Maintenance Manual. The Operations Manual contains the instructions necessary to schedule, initiate, process, and control all the jobs of a system in a production state. Job flowcharts, job initiating instructions, production schedules, and similar information are contained in the Production Folder.

• The **User Folder** contains the User's Manual and related user training materials. The User Folder also contains instructional material describing user responsibilities and procedures relative to properly entering data into the system and to utilizing its outputs.

MANAGEMENT OPTIONS

All the documents described in the previous section may not be required for every project. On a small project, types of documents may run together, with one manual containing user, operations, and maintenance documents. After determining the size and complexity of the project, the project manager must determine which documents will be required for a project (see Illustration **1-4**). The extensiveness of documentation will vary with the size and complexity of the project. The number of documents produced will be greater for large projects than for small projects.

Documentation requirements at a Data Center will vary in accordance with the projects, typified by the following:

Type I, **Feasibility Study**: Investigation of the feasibility of a proposed data processing system

Type II, **New System**: Development of a system addressing functions that have not previously been performed

Type III, **New System**: Automation of functions that are being manually performed

Type IV, **Complex System Modification**: Modification of an existing data processing system or a complex modification to such a system

Type V, **Simple System Modification:** Simple modification to an operational system

Type VI, **Emergency Program Maintenance:** Performance of emergency maintenance work on an operational system

DOCUMENTATION REQUIREMENTS FOR VARIOUS TYPES OF PROJECTS

PROJECT \ DOCUMENT	UR	PC	FS	PP	FD	DR	SS	DB	PS	PD	TP	TA	UM	OM	MM	ER
Type I Feasibility Study	x	x	x	x												
Type II New System	x	x	x	x	x	x	x	x	x	x	x	x	x	x	x	x
Type III New System	x	x	x	x	x	x	x	x	x	x	x	x	x	x	x	x
Type IV Complex System Modification	x	x	x	x	x	x	x	x	x	x	x	x	x	x	x	x
Type V Simple System Modification	x	x	x	x	x	x	x	x	x	x	x	x	x	x	x	x
Type VI Emergency Maintenance										x	x	x				

UR User Request
PC Proposal & Estimate of Cost
FS Feasibility Study
PP Project Plan
FD Functional Description

DR Data Requirements Document
SS System/Subsystem Specifications
DB Data Base Specifications
PS Program Specifications
PD Program Documentation
TP Test Plan

TA Test Analysis Report
UM User's Manual
OM Operations Manual
MM Maintenance Manual
ER Evaluation Report

Illustration 1-4.

2. INITIATION

During the initiation phase of a project, a **User Request** is defined. Then a **Proposal and Estimate of Cost** to provide service is submitted. If this proposal is accepted by the user, an overall plan should be developed to control the project. This **Project Plan** should describe individual activities comprising a project and their interrelationships.

Sometimes a **Feasibility Study** is authorized to determine whether the benefits to be derived from a proposed new system offset the development cost. If the Feasibility Study results are favorable, there is usually a progression to detailed system development.

USER REQUEST

A User Request for service is shown in Illustration **2-1**. While a user may make an oral or a written request, the latter is preferred. On this form, the user briefly describes the computer application or other service desired.

USER REQUEST FORM

Date:

Requesting Department

Requester's Name

Title

Phone Number

Project Work Request and Description:

Illustration 2-1.

PROPOSAL AND ESTIMATE OF COST

An exploratory meeting should be held with the user to review the scope of the proposed work, interfaces with related projects and systems, and the user benefits to be derived from the project. Time frames for accomplishing user objectives should be discussed and determined. At this time the expected degree of involvement of the user's data processing personnel in the project should be defined. Further meetings should be scheduled if more information is required by the analyst before a proposal can be prepared for the user.

After these initial discussions, the project analyst should prepare a proposal for the user. The development of a data processing application requires consideration of a number of factors. In determining the time and manpower resources that must be assigned to each activity, the following factors should be considered:

- The work experience and general capabilities of the personnel that can be assigned to the work

- The magnitude of the effort in terms of manpower and other resources required to complete the project

- The programming language chosen for application programming, with more programming time allowed for assembly languages than for higher level languages

- The logical structuring, file accessing, and updating complexity of the system data base

- The relative complexity and number of different types of input documents and output reports to be processed by the system

- The number of system specification changes expected during system development

- The unique requirements of on-line systems if the system to be developed will operate in an on-line environment

The Proposal and Estimate of Cost should include the following information:

- **Description of request**: This is a narrative describing the project and the objectives to be achieved.

- **Major tasks of the project**: This section will outline the work required to complete the project. It may include a Feasibility Study in addition to system design and programming, or may specify programming only.

- **Project staffing and organization**: This paragraph will describe the organization of the project, including the general number and level of competence of people to be assigned at each level. If different steps will require different types of staffing, this should be specified.

- **Customer participation**: The user's responsibility with respect to the project should be defined. This includes indicating the number of people to be assigned by the user and their level of competence. Work areas highly dependent on completion by the customer should be described.

- **Time limit for acceptance**: A final date for the user's acceptance of the proposal should be indicated.

- **Cost**: The total estimated cost of development should be indicated.

If the Proposal and Estimate of Cost is accepted, a Notice of Approval to Implement should be sent to the Data Center. Account and project identification numbers will then be assigned to the work effort. Illustration **2-2** shows a Proposal and Estimate of Cost.

FEASIBILITY STUDY

A Feasibility Study (see Illustration **2-3**) requires careful planning and a well defined approach and methodology. The time and resources needed for a substantive study as well as the importance of this type of study are frequently underestimated.

PROPOSAL AND ESTIMATE OF COST

From: Data Center Director
To: Client Department

Type of System ______________

Preliminary Estimate ______________

Final Estimate ______________

1. Development Cost

SCHEDULE

Major Project Activities	Start Date	Completion Date	Cost
1) Initiation			
2) Analysis			
3) Design			
4) Development (Programming)			
5) Implementation			
A. System Testing			
B. User Training			
6) Operation			
A. Transfer of System			
B. System Evaluation			
7) System Documentation			
8) Other			

Total
Development Cost $______________

2. Annual Operating Cost

	Cost
1) Computer Time	
2) Data Conversion	
3) System Maintenance	
4) Other	

Estimated
Annual Operating Cost $______________

Illustration 2-2.

OUTLINE FOR FEASIBILITY STUDY

SECTION 1 GENERAL

1.1 Purpose of the Feasibility Study

1.2 Project References

SECTION 2 STUDY RECOMMENDATIONS

2.1 Summary of Findings

2.2 Alternatives Considered

2.3 Study Recommendations

SECTION 3 PROPOSED SYSTEM

3.1 System Benefits

3.2 Relationship to Existing Systems

3.3 Effect on Current Operations

SECTION 4 ACTION PLAN

4.1 Decisions Required

4.2 Schedule of Activities

4.3 Resources Required

ILLUSTRATION 2-3.

The primary purpose of the Feasibility Study is usually to determine whether the value and benefits of the new system justify the costs. A well executed Feasibility Study will establish the foundation for a more detailed system study.

Notifying employees of plans to conduct a study is a management responsibility of the user, but one which is often not given sufficient attention. Top management's explicit support of, and confidence in, the study team should be communicated to the entire organization. Prior to the study, a plan of action should be prepared to reflect the desires of management and the technical requirements of the study team. Top management should clearly define the objectives and scope of the study. This definition is important because the study may cut across organizational lines, in which case the team may suggest changes in procedures, forms, reports, and organization.

Management should also set the priorities for the study. These priorities will provide the basis for the allocation and availability of resources for the study. Several specific problems can usually trigger the Feasibility Study. Management must determine the most crucial problems and establish the relative priority of each. With this information, the study team can prepare its work plan.

An initial step in conducting a study is to determine the legal limitations, policy directives, and managerial restrictions that may affect the conclusion indicated in the study. The study team will next consider the existing business operations to determine if they should be automated. For each operation, the team will document the volume of activity, frequency of processing, costs, and manpower. A total cost for the existing system operation will be developed and then will be compared with the total cost of an automated system.

Costs can also be divided into replaceable (they can be eliminated by automation) and nonreplaceable costs (they continue with the new system). The nonreplaceable costs may make it difficult to justify automating an operation solely on the basis of cost reductions.

Two general categories of benefits from automation can be distinguished -- tangible and intangible. A tangible benefit is one that can be measured and directly related to the automation of an activity. An intangible benefit is one that is difficult to measure. An improvement in customer service, made possible by a more responsive system, is an example of an intangible benefit because it is difficult to place a monetary value on the improvement of customer service. There are levels of tangibility of computer benefits, some being less tangible than others.

In the past, computer systems were justified and installed on the basis of dollar displacement. For example, a business could point to the fact that the cost of operating a computer for its inventory control functions would be more than offset by the amount of salaries otherwise needed for the inventory and supply clerks, had they not been displaced by the system. This approach was almost mandatory in justifying the high cost of programming and operating a computer. Now automated systems often cannot be justified on a tangible benefit basis. The benefits of an information system may be largely intangible. Therefore, an attempt must be made to quantify these intangible benefits to justify automation.

The final task of the study team is to organize and present the results of the study in a written report to management. This report should include the activities, findings, and recommendations of the study team. Sufficient detail should be included to permit a management decision as to whether or not to automate the operation.

The Feasibility Study should contain a concise statement of conclusions and recommendations as well as supporting material for the study. The statement of conclusions and recommendations should include not only a breakdown of costs for the present and proposed systems, but the major resources required to implement the proposed system. The study should contain a tentative timetable for proceeding with the project if the recommendations in the report support automation.

PROJECT PLAN

After a user's authorization to implement a system has been received, the assigned project manager should plan the work to be accomplished. If appropriate, bar charts or networks should be included. Utilizing the Project Plan form (see Illustration **2-4**), the project manager should assign a schedule, manpower allocation, miscellaneous costs, and operations costs to each planned activity. After the Project Plan has been approved, work on the project can commence.

Project Title ______________________

Project Manager ______________________

Type of System ______________________

Date:

ACTIVITY		TIME SCHEDULE		MANPOWER ALLOCATION		COST CODE	COST DESCRIPTION	COST
IDENTIFICATION	DESCRIPTION	START	COMPLETE	CATEGORY	HOURS			

ILLUSTRATION 2-4.

At the outset of analysis and of each task or subtask, the planning activity is performed. This is singled out as a distinct and separate activity to assure that it receives the proper emphasis and necessary investment of time. During each planning activity, the following steps will be performed:

• Review documentation of events and efforts preceding this task but having a bearing on this phase.

• Divide the current task into a series of tasks composed of related activities.

• Determine the estimated amount of effort involved in the performance of each activity and whether any specialty or background experience would aid in the performance of the work.

• Organize a checklist of activities.

• Schedule the activities by completing a Gantt chart.

• Reassess the activities to assure that all requirements for each phase are met.

• Review the schedule of activities to determine that there are no inconsistencies with the master plan. If there are, initiate immediate corrective actions by discussing the problem with the project manager.

To assure conformance with the planning activity requirements, the planning activity itself should be shown as a first item on both the Gantt chart and the checklist of activities.

The successful management of a project requires that its plan and structure be defined at its inception. If it is large enough, the project should be broken down into subunits, or modules. The subunits should then be analyzed to establish the checkpoints, or developmental milestones, necessary for project control. If possible, each milestone should have a visible output, a document or product, that clearly establishes the status and quality of work already performed on the project at that specific point in the development cycle.

Project control requires control of quality, cost, time, and resources. By using a project control system, we are seeking to answer the following questions:

Cost

- What will the total estimated costs of the project be?

- Is the actual cost of the project to date over or under the estimated cost?

Time

- What is the estimated time for completing the total project?

- Is the project behind schedule, or ahead of it?

- When should each activity start?

- What will happen to the project if the

completion of an activity is behind schedule, or ahead of it?

Resources

- How many people should be assigned to the project?

- What skills should they have?

- How should specific work assignments be made?

- What machine time and other resources are required by the project?

The project manager is responsible for the successful completion of the project. This responsibility includes developing the Project Plan that contains a description of all the activities comprising a project and their interrelationships. As part of this plan, estimates show the manpower, machine, and other resources necessary to effectively complete the project. In addition, a list of developmental milestones (review points) is prepared in order to measure the progress of the project.

Quantitative control of the project involves a comparison of budgeted versus actual manpower, machine, and cost expenditures. At review points, the actual progress of the project is compared to the estimated progress to determine whether a project is on schedule. The project control system should provide the information necessary for quantitative control of the project. Qualitative control of the project includes review of work performed in terms of accuracy, completeness and overall quality. The project manager is responsible for the qualitative review of projects to ensure that the work produced on projects is compatible with established standards. Logical control points can be utilized as checkpoints by the project manager. At each checkpoint, the progress of the project should be reviewed both quantitatively and qualitatively.

For planning and control purposes, projects can often be subdivided into the following representative tasks:

Initiation

- Receive User Request for service.
- Write Proposal and Estimate of Cost.
- Prepare Feasibility Study (optional).
- Write Project Plan.
- Obtain management's approval of the plan.
- Obtain the user's authorization to implement.

Analysis

- Study old system.
- Analyze and outline functional areas.
- Define system inputs and outputs.

- Describe functional areas.
- Isolate problems and factors by function.
- Chart flow of information and of data.
- Determine requirements of new system.
- Document system's values and benefits.
- Review with management.
- Prepare Functional Description.
- Obtain management's approval of specification.
- Try to freeze system changes.

Design

- Study Functional Description.
- Finalize required outputs.
- Finalize required files and data base.
- Finalize required inputs.
- Finalize system control procedures.
- Develop flowcharts for system.
- Develop detailed data flows of subfunctions.
- Develop detailed program runs.
- Develop detailed estimates of volume of activity for each program and frequency of processing it.

- Finalize processing requirements.
- Define system's controls and audit features.
- Define system's test requirements.
- Write conversion plan.
- Complete System Design Report.
- Obtain management's approval of report.

Development

- Study System Design Report.
- Complete block diagrams and flowcharts.
- Complete program coding.
- Complete desk checking and logic reviews.
- Complete compilation of programs.
- Develop sample test data.
- Perform simple data tests.
- Perform volume tests of program.
- Complete Program Documentation.

Implementation

- Study Program Documentation.

- Prepare Test Plan.
- Review test specifications.
- Develop system test data.
- Create test data base.
- Perform system integration tests.
- Obtain user's approval of test results.
- Prepare implementation schedule.
- Complete data conversion.
- Complete User's Manual.
- Complete user training.
- Run parallel operation.
- Obtain user's acceptance of system.
- Finalize all procedures.
- Finalize all documentation.
- Finalize all instructions.
- Monitor and check new system results.
- Adjust system to meet operating requirements.

Operation

- Prepare final Operations Manual.

- Prepare final Maintenance Manual.
- Operate live system.
- Perform post-conversion troubleshooting.
- Evaluate operational system.
- Review system modification requests.
- Implement modifications.
- Prepare Evaluation Report.

A key element in estimating time and cost is the division of large systems and programming efforts into a number of discrete activities to each of which a time and cost can be assigned. Bar charts and network planning methods provide the methodology for the division of work into discrete activities.

The primary advantage of the bar chart is that it provides a graphic means of portraying the plan, schedule, and progress of a project. As a graphic presentation device, the bar chart is especially effective in showing the status of the various elements of the project. Those elements which are behind schedule, or ahead of it, are easily and quickly identified. One needs only to note the last posting date and draw a vertical line across the chart. Progress bars not extending to this vertical line identify those elements that are behind schedule; bars extending past the vertical line identify those elements which are ahead of schedule. For the project as a whole, the length of time behind schedule is usually determined by the element with the maximum amount of delay. Similarly, the length of time ahead of schedule for the whole project would be determined by the element with the minimum amount of time ahead of schedule. Thus, for evaluation purposes, the bar chart measures the length of time behind schedule, or ahead of it, with reference to the "as of," or posting, date.

A critical path network is a graphical representation, or model, of a project. It is a means of describing the interrelationships between project tasks and of separating the planning and scheduling functions. Planning is defined as the act of stating the activities which must occur in a project and the order in which those activities are to be accomplished, based on considerations of technology and sequence only. Scheduling is defined as the act of producing project timetables, based on a plan, and the costs and time period associated with each activity. Network analysis techniques were developed for providing quantitative information to be used in scheduling the project and in forming the basis of a system for management by exception.

The following reports are representative of the types of reports that can be utilized to control a project:

- The **Project Control Report** goes to project leaders and management. This report will indicate estimated versus actual time and cost expenditures for each project activity.

- The **Production By Employee Report** shows for each employee: the projects worked on, the kind of work, and the number of hours.

- The **Summary Project Progress Report** lists projects and shows the original cost estimates for the project and actual expenditures to date.

- The **Employee Production By Work Code Report** provides information on the expenditure of manpower resources by type of work.

- The **Budget Report** shows budget allocations for the ADP Department and charges against these allocations.

3.
ANALYSIS

During the analysis phase of a project, a **Functional Description** is prepared, taking into consideration the old system, if there is one. Written in user terms, this Functional Description defines the capabilities and benefits of the system to be developed and should be formally approved by the user prior to detailed design work. An attempt should be made to minimize changes in specifications after the Functional Description has been approved. In addition, a **Data Requirements Document** may also be prepared. This document defines data elements and specifies data collection requirements.

TECHNIQUES AND TOOLS FOR ANALYSIS

Analysis for designing information systems is often overwhelming. It calls for reviewing currently used records, documents, organizational charts, and other printed materials that may contribute to a greater understanding of actual procedures and practices. Work sampling techniques and observation of working activities can be of great benefit to the analyst. Some of the analyst's work can be facilitated by the use of the following tools:

Interviews and Questionnaires

These tools are used by the analyst to gather information from the personnel who are operating and managing the existing system and from the personnel who will be affected by the new system. They provide insight into how the present system is working and the environment in which the new system must work.

Interviews are used to determine the nature of the work, relationships to other departments, the organizational structure, policies, and major functions being performed. Interviews must be carefully planned, and the results should be carefully checked and verified for accuracy and completeness.

Two types of interviews commonly used by analysts are structured interviews and general interviews. A structured interview is controlled by a set of predefined questions that guide the interview. It is normally used when several people with similar or related positions are to be interviewed either individually or in small groups in an attempt to arrive at a set of conclusions. A general interview is less formal and more flexible in structure. The format and direction of the interview session will vary greatly with the personality of each interviewer and interviewee.

Questionnaires are used for gathering facts where the analyst must contact large numbers of individuals and obtain answers to a wide variety of questions. These questionnaires must be carefully worded to elicit meaningful responses that will contribute to the study.

The system analyst must be able to prepare interview questions and questionnaires, establish rapport with interviewees, conduct interviews, and document the information obtained from the interviews. Gathering data by means of interviews is a primary method of collecting data to define user requirements. The interviewer can also win user cooperation and support for the data system to be developed by involving the user in defining specifications for the new system.

Data Forms

These forms document the following types of information:

- **Transaction Analysis** forms are used to document the flow of data between data processing systems, functional areas, and work centers by type of transaction, volume of activity, and frequency of processing.

- **File Analysis** forms produce details about data elements, volume of activity, frequency of processing, and characteristics of data elements. File analysis reveals file characteristics, file redundancies, file sizes, and file volatility.

- **Reports Analysis** forms show reports being produced and those required from the new system by type, content, and frequency of processing.

• **Work Center Analysis** forms describe transactions and required files at work centers. The information relationships between work centers are also investigated and documented.

• A **work distribution chart** provides an analysis of what jobs are being done, who performs them, and how the work is divided among individuals as a working unit. Analysis of the work distribution chart may be of value in determining if major activities have been assigned sufficient time, if excessive time is being spent on relatively unimportant functions, and if there is duplication of effort. The work distribution chart summarizes actual job duties in a form that facilitates critical questioning of existing procedures.

• A **process flowchart** breaks down and analyzes individual and successive steps in a process, identifies the various steps, and differentiates between productive and nonproductive elements. The utilization of symbols provides a clear illustration of a procedure. Supplementary information is also included to provide a brief description of each step, the time required in movement, and related information.

• A **system flowchart** describes the flow of data through all parts of a system and is used to broadly describe the steps in an application from the initial recording of data from the source document to producing the final output.

Decision Tables

These tables are used to define system logic. Decision tables are usually supplements to flowcharts and block diagrams. They define complex decision logic by showing actions to be taken, based upon a specific set of conditions.

Application Libraries

Various libraries, organizations, and vendors have publications describing applications. Professional associations can usually direct the analyst to information about specific applications.

Automated Analysis

The computer itself can be used as a valuable analytical tool. Using it for analysis can:

- Standardize and simplify collecting facts to be analyzed.

- Relieve personnel of tedious and time-consuming chores (checking, tracing, verifying, and reconciling) and permit them to perform a more comprehensive analysis.

- Relieve analysts for higher level analysis. For example, AUTOSTAT (Automated Data System Analysis Technique) was developed by RAND Corporation to employ computers for organizing facts about the work flow of documents.

Operations Research (Simulation/Models/Gaming)

Operations research can be used to produce a mathematical model of the system being developed.

This model can assist the analyst to understand the system's operation and to predict its behavior under specific conditions. Some of the benefits derived from the use of simulation, models, and gaming are:

- Predicting the proposed system's performance

- Recording the system's behavior as the environment changes

- Determining the system's performance when system variables are changed

- Predicting cost of the system relative to changes in the configuration of software and hardware

Networks (PERT/CPM)

Using networks, the analyst can study a system in terms of interrelated activities in order to determine time-dependent and critical activities. Most computer manufacturers support PERT (Program Evaluation Review Technique) and CPM (Critical Path Method) software packages. These provide the analyst with a networking capability.

FUNCTIONAL DESCRIPTION

Preparations for developing a Functional Description of a system begin with defining the system's functions, which represent the operational requirements of the system. A system must be able to receive, process, store, and produce information as required. Defining these operations is an important part of analysis because it determines the impact of the system on the organization. This is analysis at its highest level. Policy issues accompany system redesign or new system implementation, and economical considerations and trade-offs must be considered throughout system analysis and design. This operational analysis will define the overall objectives to be fulfilled by the system in relation to the operational requirements of the user organization. The efficiency of a system in performing its operations determines its effectiveness. A system will usually perform the following functions:

File Creation and Maintenance

A system may require large files of information. These files would comprise the data base of the system. The system must be able to create and maintain the data base. Information must be added to the data base, and obsolete information must be deleted from it. File creation and maintenance are essential to system operation. Inherent deficiencies in the data base structure will generate control problems. Therefore, specifications for designing the data base must take into consideration the ease of maintenance and control.

Input Editing and Translation

A system must edit incoming data transactions and perform conversions and translations. All input information, including user interrogations, should be checked for validity of format and content. Information for updating files should be checked for validity before any files are updated.

Control and detection of errors are critical to the system's operation. Errors in the data base are often difficult to pinpoint and correct. Effective screening of all input to the system will minimize the possibility that errors will enter the data base. The search for errors and discrepancies in a large data base can be difficult and costly. System integrity depends upon the effectiveness of error detection controls. Errors should be discovered before they enter the system. After errors have entered the system, they may seriously disrupt system operations.

File Searching and Analysis

A system must have the ability to search the data base for specific records. User interrogations require the retrieval of records with specific attributes. The system must search the data base, analyze the records in it, and extract those records that meet the specifications for retrieval. Information retrieval depends upon the efficiency of computer file searching and analysis.

Output Generation

A system must have the ability to produce reports and information in specified formats. The individuals using the system have an idea as to what they want to retrieve and the format in which they want it displayed. Users of the system should have some freedom in selecting data from the data base. They should be able to retrieve data and have it printed or displayed in a manner that suits their requirements.

Developing a Functional Description also involves a study of the mechanics of systems. How will the new system work? What equipment, people, and communications are required? These are some of the questions that must be asked and answered. The following information is usually necessary to describe a new system:

Data Collection

- How many types of data are collected and what are the collection points?

- Are there differences in the quality or completeness of data being collected?

- Must data be consolidated at intermediate points prior to entering the system?

- Must codes be added to the data prior to processing, and are standard codes used?

- Is the coding scheme uniform?

- Is the source document format changed during data collection?

- What are the levels of skills among personnel producing data?

- What variations are there in the volume of input transactions?

- In what form are the inputs?

- What variations are there in the frequency of input transactions?

- What parts of the system do the inputs affect?

- What is the reliability of source data?

- How effective are controls and audit procedures?

Data Editing and Error Correction

- Does editing include verification of codes, verfication of format, and verification of completeness?

- Must master files and tables be used during editing?

- Is the editing procedure completed in a single step?

- Does the editing vary due to season, peak period, or location?

- Can the corrections be made before the data has been processed by the computer?

- Does error correction require rewriting the source document?

- Is error correction performed at steps in the processing cycle?

- Is error correction performed before release of source data?

- Is it necessary to correct other data as well as the source document with the error?

- Is the sequencing code available on the source document?

- Can processing be accomplished without sequencing the source document?

- Is data on multiple documents which require correlation?

- How many different sequences are required during processing?

- How many master files must transactions be matched with during processing?

- Is the code for sequencing available on both the master file and the source documents?

- Must each transaction have a matching master record?

- Is information from sources other than the source document necessary to perform the necessary calculations?

- Are mechanical devices required to process source documents?

System Files

- How frequently are master files updated, and must all transactions for a period be available during the updating process?

- Are the transactions separated by type of transaction or time period?
- Is the master file periodically purged?
- Will new master records be added, or inactive ones deleted, before updating the file with transactions?
- Is the updating process performed on line, or is batch processing used to update files?
- Are purged records moved to a history file?
- How many records are in the files?
- How many items are in each record?
- How often are the files updated?
- How are the files maintained?
- What are the access requirements?
- Can common information in files be eliminated?
- Can files be combined?

Communications Requirements

- What communication equipment is being used now?
- Are there any special communications required for remote input, remote output, or remote inquiry?
- What kind of people are involved?

- Are the present communications adequate?

- Are inquiries received for complete master records?

- Are inquiries received for fields in a master record?

- Are inquiries received for summaries of fields in a master record?

- Are several master files required to handle certain inquiries?

- What is the desired terminal inquiry response time?

- What is the volume of activity for inquiries and the frequency of processing them?

- Are requests received for inactive historical information?

- What are the types of inquiries, and who makes these inquiries?

Processing Requirements

- What processing is required?

- What decisions are being made?

- What are the daily, weekly, bimonthly requirements and priorities?

- What are the processing frequencies?

- How long does it take to complete each operation?
- What are the peaks and valleys in the volume of processing?
- How much overtime is involved?
- Is the data processed daily, weekly, monthly, annually?

Output Data

- Are summaries prepared routinely or on demand?
- Are summaries based upon classifications coded in the source data?
- Do the reports require intermediate summaries?
- How many reports are prepared by the system daily, weekly, monthly, on demand?
- How many reports are extracted directly from source documents and directly from master files?
- Are the report sequence keys available in the source data?
- How many lines are produced per document?
- How many copies of each document are required?
- What variations are there in the volume of activity for outputs?

- What variations are there in the frequency of processing outputs?

- What is the distribution of the outputs?

- In how many cases is the same data presented in varying sequence or formats?

- Do the report users differ in the information they utilize from each report?

- Are reports reproduced by user personnel?

- Could any of the reports be replaced by terminal inquiry capability?

At the conclusion of analysis, the study team should:

- Thoroughly understand the operations of the present systems.

- Know what each transaction and data code is and how it is constructed.

- Recognize all documents and understand the information which they contain.

- Have a thorough knowledge of all the reports and outputs being produced, for whom they are prepared, and what use is made of them.

- Know all equipment currently being used.

- Know all the personnel involved in the system.

The completed Functional Description describes the existing methods and procedures and then the proposed methods and procedures. The functional capabilities of the new system are defined and include planned data inputs, outputs, and processing. Also included are not only the expected costs of developing and operating the system, but the management plan to ensure successful system development.

This technical document is written in user language because many elements of the document will be subject to review by personnel who do not have a computer background. The Functional Description should be reviewed and formally approved by the user prior to detailed system development. If the scope of the Functional Description is changed at any point during the system development phase, the document should be updated, with the changes approved by the user.

Illustration 3-1 represents an outline for a Functional Description.

FUNCTIONAL DESCRIPTION

TABLE OF CONTENTS

ILLUSTRATION 3-1.

SECTION 1. GENERAL

1.1 Purpose of Functional Description

The purpose of the FD should be described in the following words, modified as appropriate:

This Functional Description for (Project Name) (Project Number) is written to provide:

- The system requirements to be satisfied which will serve as a basis for mutual understanding between the user and the developer.
- Information on performance requirements, preliminary design, and user impacts, including fixed and continuing costs.
- A basis for the development of system tests.

1.2 Project References

A brief summary of the references applicable to the history and development of the project should be provided. The general nature of the computer programs (inventory control, management information, etc.) to be developed shall be specified. The project sponsor, user, and the operating center(s) that will run the completed computer programs should be indicated. A list of applicable documents shall be included. At least the following shall be specified by author or source, reference number and titles:

- Project request, a copy of which must be included as an appendix.
- Previously developed technical documentation relating to this project.
- Significant correspondence relating to the project.
- Documentation concerning related projects.
- Other manuals or documents that constrain or explain technical factors affecting project development.
- Standards or reference documentation, such as:
  - Documentation standards and specifications.
  - Programming conventions.
  - Hardware manuals.

SECTION 2. SYSTEM SUMMARY

This section shall provide a general description written in non-ADP language of the proposed computer application.

2.1 Background

Any information concerning the background or the uses and purposes of the system that serves to orient the reader should be included. Reference should be made to relevant higher order and parallel systems. The relationships between this project and other capabilities being developed concurrently should be described.

2.2 Objectives

Statements of the major performance requirements or goals of the system should be included. These statements should be concise and may include examples. When applicable, related events such as legislative commitment should be discussed. Any anticipated operational changes that will affect the system and its use shall be identified and the provisions within the system for including these changes should be described.

2.3 Existing Methods and Procedures

This subsection should provide a description of the current methods and procedures being employed to satisfy the existing information requirements. Both quantitative and qualitative values should be provided for:

- Organizational/personnel responsibilities.
- Equipment available and equipment required.
- Inputs and outputs (including volume and frequency)
- Deficiencies (including limitations, such as time delays)

Charts depicting the existing data flow from data acquisition through its processing and eventual output should be provided. Charts may be complemented by an explanation or other charts showing the sequence in which operational functions are performed by the user and pointing out the support of these decision making activities that the present system provides.

2.4 Proposed Methods and Procedures

A description of the proposed system and its capabilities shall be presented in this subsection. When tools, techniques or procedures from other systems will be utilized with, or will become part of, the proposed system, they should be referred to in this description.

Charts depicting the proposed data flow should be provided to present an overall view of the planned capabilities. If the proposed system eliminates or degrades any capabilities in the existing system these capabilities should be described as well as the reasons for their elimination or degradation. When appropriate, alternative methods and procedures that have been considered may be included. Charts showing the major processing steps and a chart showing the interacting organizations should be included within the following paragraphs wherever they best complement the narrative.

2.4.1 Summary of Improvements

This paragraph shall provide a qualitative and quantitative summary of the benefits to be obtained from the proposed system. The capabilities that will be satisfied by the proposed system should be explicitly identified. When a required capability is an improvement of existing methods and procedures, the extent of the anticipated improvements must be stated. Also included shall be a comparison of transaction time cycles between the existing and the proposed system. The discussion shall include:

- Functional improvements (new capabilities).
- Improvements of degree (upgrading existing capabilities).
- Timeliness (decreased response time or processing time).
- The elimination or reduction of existing capabilities that are not longer needed.

2.4.2 Summary of Impacts

This sub-section should describe the anticipated impacts and associated costs of the proposed application on the existing equipment, software, organizational, and operational environments. Impacts on the user during the development of the system shall also be noted.

2.4.2.1 Equipment Impacts

Included in this discussion shall be any required additions to or modifications of the currently available equipment.

2.4.2.2 Software Impacts.

The discussion of software impacts will include any additions or modifications needed to existing applications and support software programs in order to adapt them to the proposed application.

2.4.2.3 Organizational Impacts

Organizational impacts may include the modifications of positional responsibilities and the addition or elimination of responsibilities that will be necessary to implement the new system. Any personnel interactions eliminated will be identified and a discussion provided of the possibilities of retraining. Staff, operator, and program maintenance personnel responsibilities will be discussed. Requirements for additional personnel will be identified, including number and skills.

2.4.2.4 Operational Impacts

Operational impacts will include changes

required in both staff and operations center procedures to use the new system. This subsection should discuss impacts on the relationships of the operating center and the user; impacts on the operational procedures of the operating center; operational similarities with other systems; new data sources; quantity, type, and timeliness of data to be provided; data retention and data retrievals; methods of reporting; and results of the suspension of operations of the system by failures. An estimate of the amount of computer time needed for processing the new computer application should be included.

2.4.2.5 Development Impacts

This subsection should include a discussion of all user effort that will be required prior to installation of the application, such as manpower required to develop the data base, and operator and computer time necessary for testing. The requirement to develop conversion programs to modify existing data files to be used by the new computer programs should be identified.

Exceptional levels of manning or computer time required for the parallel operation of the new and existing systems shall be discussed.

2.5 Expected Limitations

Any limitations affecting the desired capability and explicit identification of any current or desired capabilities which will not be provided by the proposed system should be discussed in this subsection.

SECTION 3. DETAILED CHARACTERISTICS

3.1 Specific Performance Requirements

This paragraph shall describe the specific performance requirements to be satisfied by the system. The requirements will be stated in such a manner that system functions discussed in paragraph 3.2 and the system tests necessary for implementation can be related to them. A quantitative presentation can be related to them. A quantitative presentation of requirements will be included, such as the maximum allowed time from query to display of data.

3.1.1 Accuracy and Validity

This paragraph shall provide a description of the accuracy requirements placed upon the system. The following items must be considered:

- Accuracy requirements of mathematical calculations.
- Logical and legal accuracy of alphanumeric data.
- Accuracy of transmitted data.

3.1.2 Timing

This paragraph shall provide descriptions of the

timing requirements placed on the system, if they are available. The following timing requirements shall be considered:

- Throughput time.
- Response time to queries and to updates of data files.
- Response time of major functions.
- Sequential relationship of functions.
- Priorities imposed by types of inputs and changes in modes of operation.
- Timing requirements for the range of traffic load under varying operating conditions.

3.2 System Functions

This paragraph shall describe the individual functions performed by the system. This description should relate the functions to the performance requirements and to the subsystem or computer programs that will provide the functions and will show how the aggregate of these functions satisfies the specific requirements in paragraph 3.1. If an edit program is required, for example, the fields to be edited and their expected characteristics should be indicated.

3.3 Inputs/Outputs

This paragraph shall explain and show examples of the various data inputs to be used in the system. When available, the medium (disk, cards, magnetic tape), format, range of values, and accuracy, should be specified. Examples and explanations of the data outputs of the system and any quality control outputs that have been identified should be provided. Descriptions and layouts or examples of hard copy reports as well as graphic or display reports should be included. When an interactive system is being described, these outputs must be related to the system functions described in paragraph 3.2.

3.4 Data Characteristics

This paragraph shall provide discussion concerning the storage of the data elements to be used by the application. It should include information on specific data elements by name and characters, if known. Also discussed shall be dictionaries, tables, and reference files, if applicable. An estimate of total storage (number of tape files/disk modules and total number of records/cylinders) for the data and related components based on a summation of the requirements should be included. A description of the expected growth of the data and related components should be provided.

3.5 Failure Contingencies.

This paragraph shall provide a discussion of possible failures of the hardware or software system, the consequences (in terms of system performance) of such failures, and the alternative courses of action that may be taken to satisfy the information requirements. There shall be included as appropriate:

- Backup - A discussion shall be provided of the backup techniques for insuring the continued achievement of system function. "Backup" as used means the redundancy available in the event a primary system element goes down. For example, a backup technique for a disk output would be a tape output.
- Fallback - An explanation of the fallback techniques for insuring the continued satisfaction of the specific requirements of the system shall be provided. "Fallback" as used indicates the use of

another system or other means to accomplish the system requirements. For example, the fallback technique for an automated system might be manual manipulation and recording of data.

- Restart - A discussion shall be included of the restart capabilities for insuring effective and efficient recovery from a temporary problem within the hardware or software systems.

SECTION 4. ENVIRONMENT

4.1 Equipment Environment

This paragraph shall provide a description of the equipment capabilities required for the operation of the system. This paragraph will present broad descriptions of the equipment presently available and the characteristics of any new equipment necessary based on the discussions in Section 3. A guideline for equipment to be described follows:

- Processor(s), including number of each and size of internal storage.

- Storage media, including number of disk units, tape units, etc.
- Output devices, including number of each on/off-line.
- Input devices, including number of each on/off-line.
- Communications net, including line speeds.

4.2 Support Software Environment

This paragraph shall provide a description of the system software with which the computer programs to be developed must interact. This includes input and equipment simulators and test software. The correct nomenclature, level (version), and documentation references of each such software system, subsystem, and program shall be provided. In addition, the language, the operating system, and any Data Management System to be used will be identified.

4.3 Interfaces

This paragraph shall provide a description of the interfaces with other systems and subsystems. For each interface, the following shall be specified:

- Description of operational implications of data transfer, including security considerations.
- General description of data transfer requirements to and from the subject program and characteristics of communications media/systems used for transfer.
- Current formats and volume of interchanged data.
- Type of anticipated interface, such as manual or automatic.
- Anticipated interface procedures, including telecommunications considerations.

4.4 Security

This paragraph shall identify the classified components of the system including computer programs, inputs, outputs, and data bases. This paragraph will specify the level of classification of each component.

SECTION 5. COST FACTORS

The purpose of this section is to discuss cost factors that may impact upon the development, design, and continued operation of the proposed system. Alternatives that may be discussed include those for system development and system design with consideration being given to equipment, software, supporting telecommunications requirements, organization, and operation.

SECTION 6. DEVELOPMENTAL PLAN

This section shall discuss the overall management approach to the development and implementation of the proposed system. Included may be a discussion of the documentation to be produced, time frames for the development of the system or the modules of the system, necessary liaison and participation by other organizations to insure successful development, and any other factors that must be known prior to initiating development.

DATA REQUIREMENTS DOCUMENT

The Data Requirements Document (see Illustration **3-2**) is normally prepared when a data collection effort by the user organization is required to generate and maintain system files. This technical document, written in user language and prepared by both systems and user personnel, serves as a tool for developing the data processing system and for coordinating standard data elements. It is to be as detailed as possible concerning the definition of inputs required of the user, the procedures to be followed in providing these inputs to the system, the description of expected output data, specifications for all uses of standard data elements, and the data limitations of the system.

Included in this document should be the names and associated codes of data elements, standardized in order to facilitate data exchange and commonality of data structures. These standard data elements and data element codes will be used whenever applicable in all data base files.

DATA REQUIREMENTS DOCUMENT

TABLE OF CONTENTS

ILLUSTRATION 3-2.

SECTION 1. GENERAL

1.1 Purpose of Data Requirements Document

This section will describe the purpose of the Data Requirements Document in the following words, modified when appropriate:

The objectives of this Data Requirements Document for (Project Name) (Project Number) are to list and define data elements which the system must handle and to communicate data collection requirements to the user.

1.2 Project References

This part will provide a brief summary of the references applicable to the history and development of the project. The general nature of the computer programs (financial, inventory control, accounting, management information, etc.) to be developed shall be specified. The project sponsor, user, and operating center(s) that will run the completed application shall be indicated. To be included is a general statement as to the user support necessary to furnish the required system data.

Included shall be a brief statement of the project objectives and a description of the relationship of this project to other projects. A list of applicable documents shall be included. At least the following shall be specified, when applicable, by author or source, reference number, and title:

- Project Request.
- Other technical documentation.
- Functional Description.

1.3 Modification of Data Requirements

This part will describe the procedures for implementing and documenting changes to the system data requirements.

SECTION 2. DATA DESCRIPTION

The data described in this section will be separated into two categories, static data and dynamic data. Static data is defined as relatively permanent data used mainly for reference during system operation. It is generated or updated infrequently during periodic system runs. Dynamic data includes all data which is intended to be frequently updated as input to a system during a normal run or as output by the system. Both types of data are composed of data elements. The data element names listed in paragraphs 2.1, 2.2, and 2.3 shall be those contained in standard data element libraries, whenever applicable.

2.1 Logical Organization of Static System Data

This paragraph shall list the titles of static data elements used by the system for either control or reference purposes. The data elements will be arranged in logical groupings, such as functions, subjects, or other categories which are relevant to their usage.

2.2 Logical Organization of Dynamic Input Data

This paragraph shall provide a list of the titles of dynamic input data elements which constitute the data that is intended to be updated by a normal system run or during on-line operation. The data elements will be arranged in logical groupings, such as functions, subjects, or other categories which are relevant to their usage.

DR-3

2.3 Logical Organization of Dynamic Output Data

This paragraph shall provide a list of the titles of those dynamic output data elements intended to be updated by a normal system run or during on-line operation. The data elements will be arranged in logical groupings, such as functions, subjects, or other categories which are relevant to their usage.

2.4 Internally Generated Data

This paragraph will specify internally generated data of interest to the user. The elements included in this paragraph need not be all inclusive, because they will be only of informational value to the user and will require no user action.

2.5 System Data Constraints

This paragraph will contain the known or anticipated system data constraints which have not been outlined in the *Functional Description*. This information is to provide a general indication of the limits of the system with regard to future expansion or utilization; for example, a statement of the maximum size and the maximum number of files, records, and elements. Emphasis shall be placed on limits which could prove critical in future systems development.

SECTION 3. USER SUPPORT FOR DATA COLLECTION

All of the data elements required for the system will be listed in paragraphs 2.1, 2.2, and 2.3. Section 3 will describe the data collection support necessary from the user to gather the data collection support necessary from the user to gather the data values to be utilized by the system.

3.1 Data Collection Requirements and Scope

This paragraph will describe the types of information needed by the developer to establish the data values of each data element. It will specify the types of information needed to describe each data element in accordance with the information required for the data element library. It will also specify the information to be collected by the user, logically grouped and presented in a manner that will enable the user to make an effective response. The following supplementary information may be required:

A. Input Source(s) of the Data Element

This item names the source(s) from which the data element will be entered into the system. The source of the data will be specified as an operator or organizational unit--not as the hardware device used to enter the data.

B. Input Medium

This item names the hardware device used to enter data into the system. When only certain stations and devices are legal entry points, the stations and devices shall be specified.

C. Recipients

This item specifies the users (other than the originator) who should be cognizant of the data. In specifying recipients, distinctions should be made among the following classes of data elements:

- Data elements input to the system, processed by it, and output from it essentially unchanged.

- Data elements generated by a program and output to the user.
- Data elements that are input to the system but that are not output by it. In this case, the program would substitute for the user as the recipient.

D. Critical Value

Many elements that have a range of values will have one value that is particularly significant to the user. This may be a breakpoint or minimum level. When applicable, the critical value and its significance to the user should be specified.

E. Scales of Measurement

For numeric scales, if the successive steps are not equal to "one" on the units of measurement, then the increment shall be specified. For example, when utilizing numeric scales where averaging functions other than the arithmetic mean are appropriate, these other functions (e.g., geometric mean, root mean square) should be indicated. For non-numeric scales any relationships indicated by the legal values should be stated. For example, a code indicating geographical location by values A, B, C, etc. should show whether or not the value is arbitrary (A = Northeast, B= South, etc.).

F. Conversion Factors

Measured quantities that must go through digital conversion processes shall have the conversion factors specified.

G. Output Form/Device

Output data elements may be presented to the user symbolically, graphically, or may be used as input to some other automated system. This description should specify how the user will receive output data elements, for example, as part of a hard copy printout or as symbols in a CRT display. If the output is input to another automated system, the medium should be described, e.g., magnetic tape, punched cards, communications link.

H. Expansion Factors

When describing systems that are expected to undergo future expansion, the expansion factor to be added to the maximum number of entries of a data element should be included.

I. Frequency of Update

Data elements that are input to the system or that are expected to be modified by the system on a periodic basis should have the frequency of update specified. If the input arrives in a random or in an "as occurred" manner, both the average frequency and some measure of the variance should be specified.

3.2 Recommended Source of Input Data

This paragraph shall delineate the source(s) of input data. Recommendations as to who shall be responsible for providing specific data inputs should be stated. This shall include, if appropriate, recommendations regarding the establishment of a user input reporting organization. Those data inputs dependent on interfacing systems, or specific documents should be identified.

3.3 Data Collection and Transfer Procedures

Specific instructions for data collection procedures

should be stated in paragraph 3.3. These instructions should include detailed formats where applicable. Communications media and input data time constraints should be stated.

3.4 Data Base Impacts

This paragraph should describe the impacts associated with collection and maintenance of the data base on the equipment, software, organizational, operational, and developmental environments. These descriptions will amplify paragraph 2.4.2 of the Functional Description. Impacts on the system resulting from deficiencies in the data base should be stated.

4. DESIGN

In the design phase of a project, detailed specifications for the new system are prepared. Such preparation includes system flowcharts, a definition of the structure of the data base, input/output requirements, processing requirements, and program specifications. Also included are clerical procedures to pre-edit data entering the system and procedures to distribute and use output information. These design specifications represent a level of detail beyond the Functional Description. This information is collected and published in a **System Design Report.** For a large-scale system, designers will generally divide the System Design Report into separate volumes. These are usually identified as **System/Subsystem Specifications, Data Base Specifications**, and **Program Specifications**, to be discussed in this chapter.

SYSTEM/SUBSYSTEM SPECIFICATIONS

System Specifications or Subsystem Specifications may be prepared by using

Illustration **4-1** as a guide. If the system for a large project can be divided into subsystems, this same outline for specifications may be used to describe individual subsystems. A subsystem is defined as one of the components in the logical division of a system into separate components. Many systems, however, may not be logically divided into smaller components because they do not have logically distinct modules. In such cases, this outline can be used to write the System Specifications.

The requirements or functions of the new system should be described in detail. Performance requirements may include:

- Job throughput time
- Terminal response
- Priority level of each job
- System reliability requirements
- System expansion capability
- Security requirements

The ability of the data system to incorporate changes (e.g., increased workloads, new system interfaces, and additional terminals) should be defined. The system's flexibility and modularity should be described. A procedure to make changes to the system should be identified and so should all assumptions and constraints that could affect further development or operation of the system.

The logical flow of the system and all system inputs and outputs should be described in detail. System flowcharts should be employed to graphically illustrate the data flow and the relationships between logical components of the system. These flowcharts are to be supported by detailed specifications for processing, files, and input/output. Narrative descriptions should supplement the system flowcharts, when appropriate.

In summary, the System/Subsystem Specifications should depict the flow of information within the system from the inception of the computer application to the distribution of the final report to the ultimate user. Interfaces with other systems should also be described. Flowcharts of the system are used to provide a pictorial display of the system, including the sources of data entering the system as well as the files and reports created and maintained by the system.

SYSTEM/SUBSYSTEM SPECIFICATIONS

TABLE OF CONTENTS

ILLUSTRATION 4-1.

SECTION 1. GENERAL

1.1 Purpose of System/Subsystem Specifications

This section shall describe the purpose of the System/Subsystem Specifications (SS) in the following words, modified when appropriate:

> The System/Subsystem Specifications for (Project Name) (Project Number) are written to fulfill the following objectives:
>
> - To provide detailed definition of the System/Subsystem functions.
> - To communicate details of the system to project personnel.
> - To define in detail the interfaces with other systems and subsystems.

1.2 Project References

This part shall provide a brief summary of the references applicable to the history and development of the project. The project sponsor, user, and the operating center(s) that will run the completed computer programs shall be indicated. A list of applicable documents shall be included. At least the following shall be specified, when applicable, by source or author, reference number and title:

- Functional Description
- Related System/Subsystem Specifications
- Other pertinent documentation not specified in the Functional Description.

SECTION 2. SUMMARY OF REQUIREMENTS

Section 2 of the System/Subsystem Specifications shall provide a summary of the system characteristics and requirements. This section shall be an expansion of the information published in the Functional Description. Any changes to the characteristics and requirements set forth in Sections 2 and 3 of the Functional Description must be specifically identified.

2.1 System/Subsystem Description

This paragraph shall provide a general description of the system/subsystem to establish a frame of reference for the remainder of the document. Higher order and parallel systems/subsystems and their documentation will be referenced as required to enhance this general description. Included within this description shall be a diagram showing the relationship of the user organizations to the major components of the system and a diagram showing the interrelationships of the system components for the system/subsystem. These diagrams shall be based on or be updated versions of the diagrams included in paragraph 2.4 of the Functional Description.

2.2 System/Subsystem Functions

This paragraph shall describe the system/subsystem functions. There will be both qualitative and quantitative descriptions of how the system/subsystem functions will satisfy system requirements. The descriptions of the system/subsystem functions should be related to the system functions established in paragraph 3.2 of the Functional Description and be stated in such a manner that the system/subsystem environment in Section 3 can be related to them.

2.2.1 Accuracy and Validity

This paragraph shall provide a description of accuracy requirements imposed on the system/subsystem. The requirements will be related to paragraph 3.1.1 of the Functional Description.

Accuracy requirements of mathematical calculations, logical and legal accuracy of alphanumeric data, and accuracy of transmitted data should be considered.

2.2.2 Timing

This paragraph shall provide a description of the timing requirements placed on the system/subsystem.

The requirements will be related to paragraph 3.1.2 of the Functional Description. The following timing requirements may be considered:

- Throughput time.
- Response time to queries and to updates of data files.
- Response time of major system/subsystem functions.
- Sequential relationship of system/subsystem functions.
- Priorities imposed by types of inputs and changes in modes of operation.
- Timing requirements for the range of traffic load under varying operating conditions.

2.3 Flexibility

This paragraph shall provide a description of the capability to be incorporated for adapting the system/ subsystem to changing requirements, such as anticipated operational changes, interaction with new or improved systems, and planned periodic changes. Components and procedures designed to be subject to change will be identified.

SECTION 3. ENVIRONMENT

This section shall provide an expansion of the environment given in the Functional Description to reflect additional analysis of the environment. Changes in the environment that effect the scope of the project as described in the Functional Description and are the result of on-going analysis and design will be identified. These changes will be discussed in terms of the impacts on the currently available environmental components (equipment, software, etc.) as well as the impacts on estimates and functions which were based on the original planned environment.

3.1 Equipment Environment

This paragraph shall provide a description of the equipment required for the operation of the system/subsystem. Included will be descriptions of the equipment presently available as well as a detailed discussion of the characteristics of any new equipment necessary. Equipment requirements will be related to the requirements stated in paragraph 4.1 of the Functional Description. A guideline for equipment to be described follows:

- Processor(s), including number of each on/off line and size of internal storage.
- Storage media, including number of disk units, tape units, etc.
- Input/output devices, including number of each on/off line.
- Communications net, including line speeds.

3.2 Support Software Environment

This paragraph will provide a description of the support software with which the computer programs to be developed must interact. Included will be both support software and test software. The correct nomenclature and documentation references of each such software system, subsystem, and program shall be provided. Included must be a reference to the languages, the operating system, and any Data Management Syetem (DMS) to be used. This description must relate to and expand on the information provided in paragraph 4.2 of the Functional Description. If operation of the computer programs to be developed is dependent upon forthcoming changes to support software, the nature, status, and anticipated availability date of such changes must be identified and discussed.

3.3 Interfaces

This paragraph will provide a description of the interfaces with other applications or systems. The individual interfaces will be related to paragraph 4.3 of the Functional Description. For each interface, the following shall be specified:

- Type of interface, such as operator control of a terminal, program interfaces with other programs.
- Description of operational implications of data transfer, including security considerations.
- Data transfer requirements to and from the subject system/subsystem and characteristics of communications media/systems used for transfer.
- Current formats of interchanged data.

- Interface procedures, including telecommunications consideration.
- Interface equipment.

If Subsystem Specifications are being written, interfaces with other subsystems which are to be developed will be described in the same manner.

3.4 Security

This paragraph shall describe the classified components of the system/subsystem, including computer programs, inputs, outputs, and data bases. These components will be related to paragraph 4.4 of the Functional Description.

3.5 Controls

This paragraph shall provide a presentation of overall system/subsystem controls. Included in this paragraph will be controls such as record counts, accumulated counts, and batch controls. If no specific controls are to be established at the subsystem level, this should be stated.

SECTION 4. DESIGN DATA

4.1 System Logical Flow

This paragraph shall describe the logical flow of the system/subsystem. Logical flow of the system/subsystem will be presented primarily in the form of Macro Flowcharts. Flowcharts will be in sufficient detail to permit computer program design. A narrative presentation, when appropriate, will be used to supplement the flowchart. Flowcharts will provide an integrated presentation of the system/subsystem dynamics, of entrances and exits, and of interfaces with other computer programs. Flowcharts will effectively represent all modes of operations, priorities, cycles, and special handling. The flowcharts will show data flow from input, through the system/subsystem, to the generation of output.

4.2 Program Descriptions

Paragraphs 4.2.1, 4.2.2, through 4.2.n shall provide descriptions of the functions (related to paragraph 2.2 of the System/Subsystem Specifications) of the computer programs in the system/subsystem.

4.2.1 Program Description

Included in this paragraph will be a description of the inputs, outputs, and data used. Each description will include the information below, as applicable.

4.2.1.1 Inputs

Each input will be described as follows:

- Title and tag.
- Format and acceptable range of values.
- Number of items.
- Means of entry and input initiation procedures; e.g., console, card, tape.
- Expected volume and frequency, including special handling (such as queuing and priority handling) for high density periods.
- Priority; e.g., routine, emergency.
- Sources, form at source, and disposition of source document.
- Security classification of input and individual items.
- Requirements for timeliness.

4.2.1.2 Outputs

Each output will be described as follows:

- Title and tag.
- Format to include headings, line spacing, arrangement, and totals.
- Number of items.
- Preprinted form requirements.
- Means of display; e.g., CRT, printer, typewriter.
- Expected volume and frequency including special handling (such as queuing and priority handling) for high density periods.
- Priority; e.g., routine, emergency.
- Timing requirements; e.g., response time.
- Requirements for accuracy.
- User recipients.
- Security classification of output.

4.2.1.3 Data Base

Each data file, table, dictionary, or directory will be described as follows:

- Title and tag.
- Description of content.
- Number of records or entries.
- Storage, to include type of storage, amount of storage and, if known, beginning and ending addresses.
- Classification
- Data retention.

4.2.2 Program Description

This paragraph (with subsequent paragraphs as required) shall describe the second computer program in the system/subsystem using the same organization as shown in paragraph 4.2.1.

DATA BASE SPECIFICATIONS

The Data Base Specifications are prepared for programmers and/or data base managers. This technical document should be sufficiently detailed to permit program coding and data base generation. Since this document is intended to cover all types of systems, it does not make specific data or presentation formats mandatory. Developers of any given system are best qualified to devise the physical formats most useful and comprehensible to project personnel.

Data Base Specifications are generally prepared when several groups will be involved in maintaining and using a common data base. These specifications indicate the contents, the logical structure, and the updating cycle (including purge periods and frequency of processing) of each file in the system. A layout is included of the records and fields comprising each file. If a data management system is being utilized, the architecture, language interfaces, query language, and reporting capabilities of the data management system are described. Illustration **4-2** shows the outline for Data Base Specifications.

Before the files or data base of any system can be structured, the system designer must have information requirements defined. Operating management and policy management must state their information requirements so that the information elements incorporated into the data base will reflect these stated requirements. Unless the information requirements of the system are stated correctly and completely, the operational system will be unresponsive to their needs.

The relationships between the information elements in the data base must also be defined. The data base will be structured, based upon these relationships, to permit information retrieval. Unless the relationships between information elements have been correctly defined, the final system will not be responsive to user interrogations.

Definitions of information requirements and relationships should recognize both present and future needs. Awareness of anticipated requirements will permit system designers to design a system accordingly. It is mandatory that the system be designed to meet future needs because managers must operate in a changing business environment.

The definition of information requirements must also anticipate personnel changes. Management changes will, of course, create changes in information requirements. A new manager may have ideas different from those of the previous manager about the information requirements of the job. Therefore, the system designer must recognize that changes in corporate management will affect the information requirements of the organization. The system designer must construct a workable data base that is usable by managers who have widely differing information requirements.

To construct a single data base responsive to a range of information needs is difficult. The need for flexibility of design is often complicated by the complex relationships between the information elements. The structure of the data base and the format of the information records must permit flexibility of response.

The data base must be easy to maintain and must permit the rapid retrieval of information. The design for the data base must recognize the dynamic nature of an environment which will require changes in the information requirements of the system. The data base designer must combine both efficiency and flexibility.

An improperly designed data base will prevent the efficient operation of the system. Improper design will result from inadequately defined information requirements and information relationships. The data base can be developed only if the requirements for the system have been clearly defined.

A vital element in design methodology is the creation of a data element dictionary that lists all coding formats and codes. Recommended coding formats and codes for the data elements contained in the subsystem files should be described in this document. The data elements must be presented in the sequence of the data element numbers assigned. For each data element, its description includes: the number of character positions required for storage of the data element value; an indication of whether alphabetic, numeric, or alpha/numeric codes are employed; and identification of the source(s) of the coding values employed.

To provide a means of referencing the various data elements, a scheme is utilized which provides a unique identification of each data element in each application. The data elements are identified by a data element number. In one identification system, the first digit identifies the data subsystem in which the data element is employed. The second digit identifies the file within the data subsystem in which the data element is contained. The last three digits represent the data element number within the specific subsystem file. Thus, the assigned data element numbers allow ease of reference to the data elements in terms of their particular applications.

DATA BASE SPECIFICATIONS (DS)

TABLE OF CONTENTS

ILLUSTRATION 4-2.

SECTION 1. GENERAL

1.1 Purpose of the Data Base Specifications

This paragraph shall describe the purpose of the Data Base Specifications in the following words, modified when appropriate:

> The objectives of the Data Base Specifications for (Project Name) (Project Number) are to describe data base organization and to provide the basic design data necessary for the construction of the system files, tables, dictionaries, and directories.

1.2 Project References

This paragraph shall identify the project sponsor, user, and the operating center(s) that will run the completed computer programs. A list of applicable documents shall be included. At least the following shall be specified, when applicable, by source or author, reference number, title, and security classification:

- Functional Description.
- Data Requirements Document.

- System/Subsystem Specifications
- Program Specifications.

SECTION 2. DATA BASE IDENTIFICATION AND DESCRIPTION

This section shall provide all of the information necessary to identify and describe the data base being documented. It shall, in addition, contain various kinds of background information essential for proper utilization of the data base.

2.1 Data Base Identification

This paragraph shall give the code name, tag, or label by which each data base may be uniquely identified. Additional descriptive information shall also be given, whether or not it is implied in the identification code.

2.1.1 System Using the Data Base

The system of which this data base is a part shall be accurately and thoroughly identified. Included shall be the full system name; system code name; tag or label; and system model, modification, or version number. If more than one system uses this data base, each shall be identified.

2.1.2 <u>Effective Dates</u>

The first and last dates of the period during which this data base may be used with the above names system shall be given. The dates may correspond to document publication dates, program testing periods, turnover periods, turnover or delivery dates depending upon the system implementation plan. This paragraph shall also indicate whether the data base is complete or incomplete, pre- or post-system delivery to the customer, test or permanent, and whether it supersedes or will be superseded by another data base. If it supersedes another data base, the availability date of the new data base must be specified.

2.1.3 <u>Physical Description of Data Base Files</u>

The physical characteristics of the master data base file(s) and duplicate working copies shall be given. This paragraph shall include the file media (disk, drum, tape, or card deck), form of the file (symbolic or binary), and the respective codes used.

2.2 <u>Labeling/Tagging Conventions</u>

This paragraph shall define the system labeling/ tagging conventions to the programmer.

2.3 <u>Organization of the Data Base</u>

This paragraph shall provide system implementers with a single, central source of major design considerations for data base handling. The purpose of this paragraph is to promote consistency of design concerning the organization and manipulation of the physical data base files. The following information shall be given for each kind of file media (tape, drum, disk) containing the data base:

a. <u>File Design and Format</u>: The Environmental Data Tape will contain three tape files as shown below:

File #1	Tape ID Label ( )
	EOF
File #2	Directory of Reports in File #3
	EOF

File #3

Report File 2 Records per Report as follows:
Report "A" control data
Report A
Report "B" control data
Report B
Etc.

b. Design Rationale: All system tapes will contain an identification label as the first tape file. All tape loading programs will check the labels against tape identification parameters input when the system is initialized.

The second tape file will contain the labels or tags of all reports in the third file in their sequential order, and a core/peripheral storage indicator. The loader program will use this to locate reports on the tape and to construct a report storage directory table in memory.

The third tape file will contain two records per report. The first will contain detailed control data about the report; the second will contain the binary report itself. The tape loader will move the reports to their assigned peripheral storage areas, and place the contents of the control records into the permanent directory maintained in core.

c. Examples: Not applicable for this tape. In this example, the organization of this physical tape file was explained sufficiently in a. and b. above).

2.4 Special Instructions

This paragraph shall contain the instructions to be followed by all personnel who will contribute to the generation of the data base and who will use it for both testing and operational purposes. Such instructions include:

- Criteria for entering data into the data base.
- Rules and procedures to be followed when submitting data for entry into the data base.
- Identification of a data control unit.
- Formats for data description sheets and cards.
- Machine run instructions for generating, modifying, updating, or otherwise using the data base files.

  In very large systems, where the details of such instructions are extensive, this paragraph may reference sections of other programming documents (manuals or specifications) where this specific information can be found.

2.5 Support Programs Available for Handling the Data Base

In this paragraph, all of the support programs directly related to the data base shall be either referenced or discussed briefly. Descriptions shall include program name, functions, and major program operating considerations, such as operating time and hardware setup required. The detailed program specification shall also be cited. If the program is only referenced, the program name, document title, document number, and appropriate sections of the document shall be provided. Examples of such programs are:

- Assemble Common Data Pool Programs (assemble symbolic data description information into binary system format and provide a common data pool for related system programs).
- Data Base Analyzing Programs (reorganize, change, or compare data at the data-file and/or the record level).
- Storage Allocation Programs (provide efficient facilities for modifying system control data and for maintaining sets of data at an organizational level).
- Data Base Loading Programs (move or copy collections of data).
- Information Processing and Data Management Systems.

Also to be included will be EAM procedures created specifically to handle the data base.

SECTION 3. DATA DEFINITIONS

This section shall include thorough, detailed definitions and descriptions of all of the data utilized by the system. The specific details of information required for each form of data may vary from system to system and will depend on the design characteristics of the systems. The information specified below is intended to cover all kinds of systems and is not intended to be totally applicable to any one system.

3.1 Data Files

A data file is a logical arrangement of information. However, within a given system, the diverse data files may vary so widely in their logical arrangements, forms, formats, and physical media that few overall rules of composition or conventions can apply to their construction, except controlling conventions, such as the requirements that they must all bear the same type of tag or label that identifies them as files. Because of the flexibility in data file construction and utilization, each file should be defined as explicitly as possible.

Information shall include:

- File tag or label.
- Name (in full).
- A brief statement of the purpose of the file, utilization, and logical criteria used for the compilation of the file.
- The largest program entity using the file.
- Primary and secondary storage media.
- File contents and format (depending upon the complexity and size of the file, this may vary from a description of each record of the file to the broad or generic categories of information contained therein).
- The form of the contents (symbolic, binary, mixed).
- Conditions under which the file is modified or updated.
- Method of modifying of updating the file.
- Restrictions and limitations on usage.
- File control information used by programs, such as storage control items, directories, pointers.

3.2 Tables

An adequate table definition shall contain the following information as applicable to the data base.

- Table tag or label.
- Full name or purpose of the table.
- Data file containing the table.
- Program subsystem that uses this table.
- Logical divisions within table (internal table blocks or parts - not entries).
- Basic table structure (fixed or variable length, fixed or variable entry structure).

  A. If fixed length table:

  - Number of words/characters per entry.
  - Number of entries in table.

  B. If variable length table:

  - Maximum length (number of words/characters).
  - Maximum number of entries (if entry structure is fixed).
  - Number of kinds of entries.
  - Key and control items of each kind of entry.

- Indication of presence or absence of table control information.
- Other directly related tables plus a statement of the relationship.
- Details of the structure of each entry type including the tag or label of each item plus its entry position; for example, word/character number or bit position.
- Unique or significant characteristics, such as: "To be loaded into hardware protected registers only", or "Contents adapted to each installation" (for a multi-site system).

3.3 Items

As used in this paragraph, the word "item" refers to a specific category of detailed information that has a defined position within a table, or is a discrete data entity (simple item), for direct and immediate manipulation by a program. Used in this sense, the definition of an item is machine and program oriented rather than operationally oriented. Item definitions shall include:

- Tag or label.
- Purpose of the item (a brief statement referenced to related data elements, when applicable).
- Table in which it is found.
- Table type in which it is found.
- Position in table (word number and bit positions/ level numbers/etc.).
- Item use; e.g., table control item, entry structure key item, string control item, data item.
- Item type; e.g., symbolic character, integer, fraction, mixed number (fixed or floating point), string.
- Item coding, depending upon the item type; for example:
    - Symbolic - character code used.
    - Integer - binary or binary coded decimal.
    - Fraction - scaling factor.
    - Mixed number, fixed point - point position.
    - Status - the maximum number of conditions, form of status values (symbolic or numeric binary), a list of all acceptable status values or conditions.
- Accessibility factor - coded to indicate machine instruction modifiers that can expedite retrieving

DS-12

and storing of the item; e.g., FW (full word), LHW or RHW (left- or right-hand word), B (byte size), M (mask necessary).

3.4 Records and Entries

Frequently, the basic unit of the data file is a record or an entry. These data units shall be defined to the same extent as tables (see paragraph 3.2). The following information for each data unit shall be given:

- Full name and purpose.
- An explanation of each item.
- Maximum size.
- Graphic representation as it is contained in the file, and examples of the output obtained from the file with significant output editing features.

SECTION 4. DATA BASE STORAGE

This section shall contain the internal and peripheral storage assignments for all of the programs and data of a system. In addition, it will contain information relevant to certain constraints and conditions under which the programs must operate. These constraints exist to ensure efficient utilization of the storage media and the computer hardware and software.

4.1 Internal Storage Map for the System

This paragraph shall include either descriptive statements or graphic representations showing the utilization of internal storage. It shall include, as applicable, areas set aside for the residence of permanent programs and data (program "overlay" areas and data "scratch" or working areas). This paragraph shall also contain a brief statement of the system design considerations that resulted in this internal storage utilization.

4.2 Storage

This paragraph, when applicable, shall list, by device and sequential storage area, all internal and peripheral storage assignments for both programs and data. The storage listing for each device shall state all addresses, areas, blocks, for the following:

- Permanent program and data storage assignments.
- Temporary program and data storage assignments, including overlays.
- Areas reserved for special purposes such as testing, experimental, or emergency use.
- Scratch or working areas.
- Unused areas.

SECTION 5. COMMON DATA POOL

If the data base is oriented to using a common data pool, this section should specify its file name and the conventions for its use.

PROGRAM SPECIFICATIONS

The Program Specifications define in detail each computer program that must be developed for a system (see Illustration **4-3**). Programmers work directly from this document when writing programs.

Each type of input and output applicable to the program is described in these specifications. The structure of the files or data bases used by the program is also defined. The processing, or logical and arithmetic, operations to be performed by the program are stated in narrative form and supported by macro logic flowcharts. The narrative and flowcharts are related to the system functions described in the Functional Description.

The program functions should be stated in sufficient detail to minimize the need for contact between the programmer and the user. Accounting type data controls are specified where appropriate to permit the computer to detect error conditions. The hardware and software environment in which the program must operate is identified and so are the interfaces between the program and other systems and programs.

PROGRAM SPECIFICATIONS

TABLE OF CONTENTS

ILLUSTRATION 4-3.

SECTION 1. GENERAL

1.1 Purpose of Program Specifications

This paragraph will describe the purpose of the Program Specifications in the following words or appropriate modifications thereto:

> The objective of the Program Specifications for (Project Name) (Project Number) is to describe the program design in sufficient detail to permit program production by the programmer/coder.

1.2 Project References.

This paragraph shall provide a brief summary of the references applicable to the history and development of the project. The project sponsor, user, and operating center(s) that will run the completed computer programs shall be indicated. A list of applicable documents shall be included. At least the following shall be specified, when applicable, by source or author, reference number, and title:

- Functional Description.

- Associated System/Subsystem Specifications.
- Related Program Specifications.
- Any other pertinent documentation.

SECTION 2. SUMMARY OF REQUIREMENTS

2.1 Program Description

This paragraph shall provide a general description of the program to establish a frame of reference for the remainder of the document. It shall include a summary of the system requirements contained in Section 2 of the System/Subsystem Specifications. The documentation of higher order systems/subsystems and related programs will be referenced, as required, to enhance the general description of the program. If the program is common to more than one system or subsystem, appropriate references will be made to the applicable System/Subsystem and Functional Description documents.

2.2 Program Functions

This paragraph shall describe the functions of the program. These shall be taken directly from those portions of the System/Subsystem Functions (paragraph 2.2 of the System/Subsystem Specifications) or the System Functions (paragraph 3.2 of the Functional Description) which apply to the subject program. The functions of the program may be described in relation to the specific requirements they satisfy if this information will enhance a description of the functions. The specific requirements may be taken from the Specific Performance Requirements (paragraph 3.1 of the Functional Description) which apply to the subject program. There will be both qualitative and quantitative descriptions of how the program satisfies the functions. If a program does not in itself satisfy system or subsystem functions, this fact shall be noted in the presentation with a statement showing how the aggregate of programs completely satisfies the functions.

2.2.1 Accuracy and Validity

This paragraph shall provide a description of accuracy requirements imposed on the program. The requirements will be related to paragraph 3.1.1 of the Functional Description or to paragraph 2.2.1 of the System/Subsystem Specifications. Changes in the accuracy requirements from the next higher order document will be identified. The following accuracy requirements must be considered:

- Accuracy requirements of mathematical calculations.
- Logical and legal accuracy of alphanumeric data.
- Accuracy of transmitted data.

2.2.2 Timing

This paragraph shall provide a description of the timing requirements placed on the program, if they are applicable. The requirements will be related to paragraph 3.1.2 of the Functional Description or to paragraph 2.2.2 of the System/Subsystem Specifications. Changes in the timing requirements from the next higher order document will be identified. The following timing requirements may be considered:

- Throughput time.
- Response time to queries and to updates of data files.
- Response time of major program functions.
- Sequential relationship of program functions and data flows.
- Priorities imposed by types of inputs and changes in modes of operation.
- Timing requirements for the range of traffic load under varying operating conditions.
- I/O transfer time required for disk, drum, tape, etc.
- Internal processing time.

2.3 Flexibility

This paragraph shall provide a description of the capability to be incorporated for adapting the program to changing requirements, such as anticipated operational changes, interaction with new or improved programs, and planned periodic changes. Components and procedures designed to be subject to change will be identified. This paragraph will be related to the portions of paragraph 2.3 of the System/Subsystem Specifications that are applicable to the subject program.

SECTION 3. ENVIRONMENT

Changes in the environment that affect the scope of the project as described in the Functional Description will be identified within the appropriate paragraphs of this section. These changes will be discussed in terms of their impacts on the currently available environmental components (software, hardware) as well as their impacts on estimates and functions which were based on the original planned environment.

3.1 Support Software Environment

This paragraph shall provide a description of the support software with which the computer programs to be developed must interact. Included will be both support software and test software. The correct nomenclature and documentation references of each such software system, subsystem, and program shall be provided. Included must be a reference to the languages and to the operating system to be used. This description must relate to and expand on the information provided in paragraph 4.2 of the Functional Description and paragraph 3.2 of the System/Subsystem Specifications. If the operation of the computer programs to be developed is dependent upon forthcoming changes to support software, the nature, status, and anticipated availability date of such changes must be identified and discussed.

3.2 Interfaces

This paragraph shall provide a description of the interfaces with other applications and computer programs. The individual interfaces will be related to paragraph 4.3 of the Functional Description and paragraph 3.3 of the System/Subsystem Specifications. For each interface, the following shall be specified:

- Type of interface, such as operator control of a terminal or program interfaces with other programs.
- Description of operational implication of data transfer, including confidentiality considerations.
- Data transfer requirements to and from the subject program (including data content, sequence, timing, format, volume, and processing), and characteristics of communications media/systems used for transfer.
- Current formats of interchanged data.
- Interface procedures, including telecommunications considerations.
- Interface equipment
- Data conversion requirements.

3.3 Storage

This paragraph shall provide a description of storage requirements for the program. Included shall be internal and auxiliary storage (tape, disk, drum) requirements and the estimated quantity of storage required for each. Each type of program must give consideration to the following types of information for the various storage media:

- Internal storage, number of words/auxiliary core bank or bytes/auxiliary core bank, number of banks.
- Drum storage, number of words/field, number of fields/drum, number of drum assemblies.
- Disk storage, number or words/zone or bytes/cylinder, number of zones/disk or cylinders/disk, number of disks/disk unit, number of disk units.
- Tape storage, number of adapters, number of tape drives/adapter, number of tapes.

In addition, the machine storage will be further allocated into permanent and temporary areas.

3.4 Security

This paragraph shall describe the classified components of the program including the computer program itself, inputs, outputs, and data bases. These components will be related to paragraph 4.4 of the Functional Description and paragraph 3.4 of the System/Subsystem Specifications.

3.5 Controls

This paragraph shall provide a presentation of program controls. Included in this paragraph will be controls such as record counts, accumulated counts and batch controls. These controls will be related to that portion of paragraph 3.5 of the System/Subsystem Specifications that relates to the program being described. If no specific controls are to be established at the program level, this should be so stated.

SECTION 4. DESIGN DATA

4.1 General Operating Procedures

This paragraph shall provide a general description of the system operating procedures. There will be a description of the load, start, stop, recovery, and restart procedures. Any special program requirements necessary for the implementation of these operating procedures shall be specified. Also discussed shall be the interaction of all programs with executive support programs.

4.2 Inputs

This paragraph shall provide a detailed description of all computer program inputs. There shall be a description of each type of input applicable to the program. Each input should be described in detail and include the following:

- Title and tag
- Format and acceptable range of values.
- Number of items.
- Description of each item to include number and type of characters (numeric, alpha, decimal, signed, unsigned), range of values, accuracy requirements.
- Means of entry and initiation procedures

- Length of input including special handling requirements due to variations in length.
- Expected volume and frequency including special handling (such as queuing and priority handling) for high density periods.
- Priority (routine, emergency).
- Sources, form at source, and disposition of source document.
- Disposition other than processing (logging, hard copy reproduction of input, storage location).
- Confidentiality classification of input and individual items.
- Flexibility, such as capability of omitting and adding items.
- Requirements for timeliness
- Throughput time.
- Special handling, such as specification of special control cards.

This paragraph shall include examples of prepared inputs and preparation forms, such as input creation sheets and communications message forms.

4.3 Outputs

This paragraph shall provide a detailed description of all program outputs. There shall be included a description of each type of output applicable to the program. Each output shall be categorized by type and described in detail to include the following as applicable:

- Title and tag
- Format to include headings, line spacing, arrangement, totals, etc.
- Number of items.
- Description of each item to include number and type of characters (alpha, numeric, symbol), range of values, accuracy requirements.
- Data selection criteria will be presented to establish the basis for selecting information for display.
- Description of plots or graphic displays will include the coordinates to be used, symbols to be used, type of graphic technique.
- Preprinted form requirements.
- Means of display (CRT, printer, typewriter, card punch).
- Expected volume and frequency, including special handling (such as queuing and priority) for high density periods.
- Priority (routine, emergency).
- Timing requirements (response time).
- User recipients and use of displays.
- Disposition, including logging, film and hard copy printout reproduction and storage, numbers of copies required for distribution, place of storage, person responsible for permanent copy, retention period, and special handling required because of confidentiality.
- Confidentiality classification of outputs and individual items.
- Explanation of symbols.
- Conditional and status indicators (code and conditional) definition.

Included in this paragraph shall be examples of program outputs.

PS-11

4.4 Data Environment

This paragraph shall provide a description of the data environment of the program. There shall be included descriptions of the files, tables, dictionaries, program interrelationship with the tables, storage allocation, intermediate data structures, and data retention requirements. The structure of a common data base may be defined here. Each program related file, table, dictionary, or directory will be described in detail to include the following, when available:

- Title and tag.
- Description of content.
- Parameters - start of file, end of file.
- Number of records or entries.
- Record parameters - start of record, end of record.
- Relationship of each record to the common data base, if applicable.
- Storage, to include type of storage, amount of storage and, if known, beginning and ending addresses.
- Normal sort order of the file and other orders required for special purposes.
- Confidentiality.

4.4.1 Storage Allocation

Storage allocation will be described for internal and auxiliary storage as follows:

- Storage media
- Available storage on each medium
- Addresses of available storage
- Erasable working storage.

4.4.2 Data Retention

Data retention requirements will be described as follows:

- Historic retention to include collection of data to be retained, format, storage medium, and time parameters.
- Periodic report data to include time retained after report generation and time retained to provide summary reports.
- Summary report data, such as time retained after summary report.

4.4.3 Program Relationships

Interrelationships of a program with the data

base(s) will be described to show the files and tables used in each program function.

4.5 Program Logic

This paragraph shall describe the logic of the program. Logical flow will be presented primarily in the form of flowcharts. A narrative presentation, when appropriate, will be used to supplement the flowcharts. All flowcharts will be keyed to the higher order flowcharts in the System/Subsystem Specification, if applicable, or the Functional Description.

The logical flow shall provide a detailed description of the processing performed by the program. There shall be included for each program function noted in paragraph 2.2 of the Program Specifications a description of the operation of the program. All processes will be described to include algorithmic logic data manipulations and decision processes involved. Conditions being tested for purposes of branching will be explained in detail, as well as methods for identifying error conditions and the resulting actions of the program.

The flowcharts and narrative will be related to the information in paragraph 4.1 of the System/Subsystem

Specification. Although the information will be more detailed, it must be relatable to any previously published documentation. Changes in the logical flow which have occurred will be explicitly identified and the reasons for the changes stated. These flowcharts will be reviewed by the programmer during the development phase and used to design the necessary computer programs. They will be a primary reference for the programmer relative to the logic structure of programs.

5. DEVELOPMENT

During the development phase, programmers write and document the computer programs specified for a system during the design phase of implementing a computer application. Program Documentation is the product of this phase.

PROGRAMMER'S TASKS

A programmer begins by reviewing the Program Specifications and then preparing logic flowcharts that depict the sequence in which a program's functions are to be performed. The program logic is organized into a series of subroutines, or modules. Then the program is coded. This entails writing instructions so that the computer performs the logic and arithmetic operations depicted in the logic flowchart. After the coded program has been desk checked for accuracy, it is compiled and machine tested to isolate undetected errors.

A programmer completes the necesssary tasks for a computer application project in the following sequence:

- Review Program Specifications.
  - Check for completeness.
  - Check for clarity.
- Construct logic flowcharts.
  - Prepare macro flowcharts.
  - Prepare micro flowcharts.
- Prepare and desk check source program.
  - Code.
  - Check coding.
  - Check logic.
- Prepare source program for computer use.
  - Compile.
  - Perform error checks.
  - Produce object program.
- Machine test program as a unit.
  - Run sample data.
  - Correct errors.
- Complete documentation.

PRODUCTIVITY TECHNIQUES

During the development phase, many organizations are now employing so-called productivity techniques. Although these techniques are relatively old in terms of concept, their use together is a recent innovation. Results on projects where they have been used are so marked that there is now a rapidly growing acceptance of these techniques throughout the industry. IBM systematically uses many of them as corporate standards. The IBM System Science Institute places emphasis on the importance of employing these techniques. Several facilities and resource management firms now utilize some or all of the techniques. These productivity techniques include top-down development, HIPO, chief programmer teams, development support libraries, structured programming, composite design, and structured walk-throughs, which are discussed separately in the following paragraphs.

Top-down Development

A phased project structure is just one aspect of top-down development. The technique of top-down development requires that implementation of the data system proceed downward from the top, with program stubs simulating the presence of modules not yet developed. Top-down development follows the natural sequence of system design and requires that definition proceed from the control (interface) architecture and basic definitions downward to the functional units of the system. With interfaces defined prior to the development of subsystems, this process produces a continual integration and testing of the system's components as they are programmed.

The traditional process of system development usually produces unplanned difficulties during system testing and integration. Too many potential sources of problems make it difficult to isolate a problem. Delays in completing a project may be due to the need for tracing and isolating a problem and then modifying a program. Management control is generally ineffective during much of the traditional process because there is no coherent, visible product until integration. These difficulties are minimized by top-down development.

HIPO

HIPO, an acronym for Hierarchy plus Input-Process-Output, is a modern form of system flowchart and program flowchart. HIPO charts are easy to change and maintain. They are understandable even by non-ADP personnel after a short introduction. A detailed HIPO chart always shows input on the left side of the chart, the processing in the center, and all output (even temporary internal computational results) on the right side. These conventions are easily grasped and accepted.

By incorporating the use of HIPO charts from the very beginning of system design, the charts prepared for the Functional Description during the analysis phase can ordinarily be used unaltered for a subsystem during the design and development phases. Even when these charts must be carried to a level of greater detail, the effort required is considerably less than that required to prepare a detailed flowchart for a program in the traditional manner.

As an indication of the value of HIPO, it can be noted that many of the more progressive data processing organizations have incorporated HIPO as the standard charting method to be used. For example, IBM now uses HIPO for all of its internal and external charting documentation.

Chief Programmer Team

A chief programmer team represents a new approach to production programming. This team uses a development support library (DSL) where a librarian maintains all programs under development in a visible, standardized form. In addition to employing structured programming to define a top-down sequence for creating and testing a program unit, the team adheres to technical standards for coding each unit.

The nucleus of a chief programmer team consists of a chief programmer, a backup programmer, and a librarian. This nucleus provides management with continuity for programming expertise and for project recording and documentation. The requirements for additional personnel will be defined by the chief programmer. A typical team will involve three to five programmers, a librarian, and other specialists. A project officer may be part of a team to help the chief programmer with administrative and personnel matters, thus allowing the latter to concentrate on the project's technical management.

The chief programmer is the technical manager to whom all team members report directly, but has the primary job of designing and coding programs. The chief programmer codes vital segments of the programming system and assigns programs to other team members to complete by using structured programming techniques. All programs are integrated into the system being developed under the supervision of the chief programmer. The backup programmer is a peer of the chief programmer in program design and development and is involved in all key work. The former can assume the leadership role at any time.

Development Support Libraries

A support librarian is accountable for documentation and support team operations. During design efforts, the support librarian keeps documentation current and coordinated. During programming, the support librarian also has the responsibility for defining data, naming data, and sometimes for coding and testing the data subroutines, or modules. During testing, the support librarian is responsible for scheduling and distributing tests and test results. The support librarian is also responsible for setting up job control and for cataloging completed programs.

The support librarian is sometimes the only team member who is allowed to code the data base definitions for the data divisions of programs. One set of these and a standard group of input/output modules for the data base will be written and catalogued by the support librarian. Other team members then **COPY** and **CALL** these modules in their programs. This approach provides the system with data base standardization.

Structured Programming

Structured programming is a discipline which guides the programmer in the development of computer programs. This discipline can improve the correctness, readability, and maintainability of a program.

It is possible to write any program by using only three structures:

- Simple sequence: In the absence of instructions to the contrary, statements are executed in the order written.
- IF-THEN-ELSE: Combine with statement brackets so that groups of statements can be included in THEN and ELSE clauses. THEN and ELSE clauses may contain any of the three structures.
- A loop control mechanism such as DO-WHILE and DO-UNTIL.

Any combination of decisions can be accommodated with one of these control structures or a combination of these structures. Each structure is characterized by a single point of entry and a single point of exit. These structures form a program which is simple in that control flows from top to bottom or from beginning to end. The control structures can be nested, but they retain their single-entry/single-exit construction. The three control structures can be constructed in any programming language.

Structured programming, combined with practices such as good annotation and descriptive labels in the source code, simplifies source coding. The reduced complexity of a structured program means that its correctness is more easily proved than that of an unstructured program. Inasmuch as the flow of control is simpler in a structured program, the development and execution of test cases to debug the program are simpler. The program is more understandable, and its correctness will be more easily proved by desk checking.

Composite Design (Modular Programming)

This program design technique is an extension of structured programming. It is a functional approach to program design that can be used by a chief programmer, or any other programmer, in determining the organization and logical partitioning of work within the programming activity.

The primary goal in designing a modular program is to decompose the program so that the modules are highly independent. Module independence is based upon the characteristics of module coupling and module strength. Modular programming design attempts to minimize the relationships among modules (module coupling) and to maximize the relationships among the parts of each module (module strength).

Module strength is a measure of the relationships among the parts of modules that perform specific, well-defined functions. A module that performs one well-defined function is a strong module.

Structured Walk-throughs

The structured walk-through is a technique requiring an analyst to make a formal presentation of his work before a group of his associates. Prior to a major event, documentation is supplied to each person who will attend the walk-through.

There are many advantages to the structured walk-through. With the prospect of being "onstage," the presenter is inclined to do a better job of desk checking prior to the walk-through. He must provide the attendees with enough information for them to appreciate the problems. Therefore, he will probably emphasize accurate documentation. The walk-throughs familiarize several members of an organization with a technical project so that the organization develops some protection in the event of personnel turnover.

At these sessions the presenter may gain knowledge and technical solutions that will improve his own productivity. Inconsistencies and misunderstandings of detailed specifications are often discovered during these walk-throughs. The time expended in the involvement of associates during the structured walk-through is usually offset by improved productivity, shorter test times, and the dissemination of good programming practices.

All of these improved techniques for programming bring the following benefits to an organization:

- Better understanding between user and technical groups
- Better communication among project personnel
- Better backup in case of personnel turnover
- More consistent quality of products
- More effective and more efficient use of experience and talents

- Improved final documentation and easier maintenance of programs

- Improved project control

PROGRAM DOCUMENTATION

Program documentation is outlined in Illustration **5-1.** It consists of the general operating procedures, inputs, outputs, narrative descriptions, layouts for files, logic flowcharts, source listings, and test results produced by programmers during program development.

The purpose of this documentation is to simplify operation and maintenance of the program by clearly defining its structure and operating characteristics. The software environment (operating system, data management system, communications software) necessary for operations of the program is described. The hardware environment (internal storage, auxiliary storage on tape, disk, or drum) required by the program is defined. This documentation also includes a description of the program's operating characteristics relative to load, start, stop, recover, and restart procedures.

A source listing of the debugged program is included wih this documentation to facilitate checking sections of the source code. In addition, the documentation contains a listing of test results to show that the program was machine tested prior to its release for operation.

PROGRAM DOCUMENTATION

TABLE OF CONTENTS

ILLUSTRATION 5-1.

SECTION 1. GENERAL

1.1 Purpose of Program Documentation

This paragraph will describe the purpose of the Program Documentation in the following words or appropriate modifications thereto:

> The objective of this Program Documentation (Project Name) (Project Number) is to describe the program in sufficient detail to permit program operation and maintenance.

1.2 Project References

At least the following shall be specified, when applicable, by source or author, reference number, and title:

- Functional Description
- Associated System/Subsystem Specifications
- Data Requirements Document
- Data Base Specifications
- Related Program Specifications
- Any other pertinent documentation

SECTION 2. GENERAL PROGRAM DESCRIPTION

2.1 Program Narrative

This paragraph shall provide a general description of the program to establish a frame of reference for the remainder of the document. It shall include a summary of the requirements contained in the Program Specifications and the System/Subsystem Specifications. The documentation of higher order systems/subsystems and related programs will be referenced, as required, to enhance the general description of the program. If the program is common to more than one system or subsystem, appropriate references will be made to the applicable System/Subsystem and Functional Description documents.

2.2 Program Functions

This paragraph shall describe the functions of the program. These shall be taken directly from the Program Specifications. The functions of the program may be described in relation to the specific requirements they satisfy if this information will enhance a description of the functions. There will be both qualitative and quantitative descriptions of how the program satisfies the functions. If a program does not in itself satisfy required functions, this fact shall be noted in the presentation with a statement showing how the aggregate of programs completely satisfies the functions.

2.2.1 Accuracy and Validity

This paragraph shall provide a description of accuracy requirements satisfied by the program. The requirements will be related to the Program Specifications. The following accuracy requirements should be considered:

- Accuracy requirements of mathematical calculations.
- Logical and legal accuracy of alphanumeric data.
- Accuracy of transmitted data.

2.2.2 Timing

This paragraph shall provide a description of program timing requirements. The requirements will be related to the Program Specifications. The following timing requirements may be considered:

- Throughput time.
- Response time to queries and to updates of data files.
- Response time of major program functions.
- Sequential relationship of program functions and data flows.
- Priorities imposed by types of inputs and changes in modes of operation.
- Timing requirements for the range of traffic load under varying operating conditions.
- I/O transfer time required for disk, drum, tape, etc.
- Internal processing time.

2.3 Flexibility

This paragraph shall provide a description of the capability to be incorporated for adapting the program to changing requirements, such as anticipated operational changes, interaction with new or improved programs, and planned periodic changes. Components and procedures designed to be subject to change will be identified. This paragraph will be related to the Program Specifications.

SECTION 3. ENVIRONMENT

The environment in which the program will operate will be defined.

3.1 Support Software Environment

This paragraph shall provide a description of the support software with which the computer programs to be developed must interact. Included will be both support software and test software. The correct nomenclature and documentation references of each such software system, subsystem, and program shall be provided. Included must be a reference to the languages and to the operating system to be used. This description must relate to and expand on the information provided in the Program Specifications. If the operation of the computer program is dependent upon forthcoming changes to support software, then the nature, status, and anticipated impact of such changes must be identified and discussed.

3.2 Interfaces

This paragraph shall provide a description of the

interfaces with other applications and computer programs. For each interface, the following shall be specified:

- Type of interface, such as operator control of a terminal or program interfaces with other programs.
- Description of operational implication of data transfer, including confidentiality considerations.
- Data transfer requirements to and from the subject program (including data content, sequence, timing, format, volume of transfer, and frequency of processing), and characteristics of communications media/systems used for transfer.
- Current formats of interchanged data.
- Interface procedures, including telecommunications considerations.
- Interface equipment.
- Data conversion requirements.

3.3 Storage

This paragraph shall provide a description of storage requirements for the program. Included shall be internal and auxiliary storage (tape, disk, drum) requirements and the estimated quantity of storage required for each. Included will be:

- Internal storage, number of words/auxiliary core bank or bytes/auxiliary core bank, number of banks.
- Drum storage, number of words/field, number of fields/drum, number of drum assemblies.
- Disk storage, number or words/zone or bytes/cylinder, number of zones/disk or cylinders/disk, number of disk/disk unit, number of disk units.
- Tape storage, number of adapters, number of tape drives/adapter, number of tapes.

In addition, the machine storage will be further allocated into permanent and temporary areas.

3.4 Security

This paragraph shall describe the classified components of the program including the computer program itself, inputs, outputs, and data bases. These components will be related to the Program Specifications.

3.5 Controls

This paragraph shall provide a presentation of program controls. Included in this paragraph will be controls such as checkpoint/restart, record counts, accumulated counts, and batch controls. These controls will be related to the Program Specifications for the program being described. If no specific controls are to be established at the program level, this should be so stated.

SECTION 4. DESIGN DATA

4.1 General Operating Procedures

This paragraph shall provide a general description of the system operating procedures. There will be a description of the load, start, stop, recovery, and restart procedures. Any special program requirements necessary for the implementation of these operating procedures shall be specified. Also discussed shall be the interaction of all programs with executive support programs.

4.2 Input Layouts

This paragraph shall provide a detailed description of all computer program inputs. There shall be a description of each type of input applicable to the program. Each input should be described in detail and include the following:

- Title and tag.
- Format and acceptable range of values.
- Number of items.
- Description of each item to include number and type of characters (numeric, alpha, decimal, signed, unsigned), range of values, accuracy requirements.
- Means of entry and initiation procedures.
- Length of input including special handling requirements due to variations in length.
- Expected volume of inputs and frequency of processing including special handling (such as queuing and priority handling) for high density periods.
- Priority (routine, emergency).
- Sources, form at source, and disposition of source document.

- Disposition other than processing (logging hard copy reproduction of input, storage location).
- Confidentiality classification of input and individual items.
- Flexibility, such as capability of omitting and adding items.
- Requirements for timeliness.
- Throughput time.
- Special handling, such as specification of special control cards.

This paragraph shall include examples of prepared inputs and preparation forms, such as input creation sheets and communications message forms.

4.3 Output Layouts

This paragraph shall provide a detailed description of all program outputs. There shall be included a description of each type of output applicable to the program. Each output shall be categorized by type and described in detail to include the following as applicable:

- Title and tag.
- Format to include headings, line spacing, arrangement, totals, etc.
- Number of items.
- Description of each item to include number and type of characters (alpha, numeric, symbol), range of values, accuracy requirements.
- Data selection criteria will be presented to establish the basis for selecting information for display.
- Description of plots or graphic displays will include the coordinates to be used, symbols to be used, type of graphic technique.
- Preprinted form requirements.
- Means of display (CRT, printer, typewriter, card punch).
- Expected volume of outputs and frequency of processing, including special handling (such as queuing and priority) for high density periods.
- Priority (routine, emergency).
- Timing requirements (response time).
- User recipients and use of displays.

- Disposition, including logging, film and hard copy printout reproduction and storage, numbers of copies required for distribution, place of storage, person responsible for permanent copy, retention period, and special handling required because of confidentiality.
- Confidentiality classification of output and individual items.
- Explanation of symbols.
- Conditional and status indicators (code and conditional) definition.

Included in this paragraph shall be examples of program outputs.

4.4 <u>Data Environment</u>

This paragraph shall provide a description of the data environment of the program. There shall be included descriptions of the files, tables, dictionaries, program interrelationship with the tables, storage allocation, intermediate data structures, and data retention requirements.

The structure of a common data base may be defined here. Each program-related file, table, dictionary, or directory will be described in detail to include the following, when available:

- Title and tag.
- Description of content
- Parameters - start of file, end of file.
- Number of records or entries.
- Record parameters - start of record, end of record.
- Relationship of each record to the common data base, if applicable.
- Storage, to include type of storage, amount of storage and, if known, beginning and ending addresses.
- Normal sort order of the file and other orders required for special purposes.
- Confidentiality.

4.4.1 Storage Allocation

Storage allocation will be described for internal and auxiliary storage as follows:

- Storage media

- Available storage on each medium
- Addresses of available storage
- Erasable working storage.

4.4.2 Data Retention

Data retention requirements will be described as follows:

- Historic retention to include collection of data to be retained, format, storage medium, and time parameters.
- Periodic report data to include time retained after report generation and time retained to provide summary reports.
- Summary report data, such as time retained after summary report.

4.4.3 Program Relationships

Interrelationships of a program with the data base(s) will be described to show the files and tables used in each program function.

4.5 Program Logic

This paragraph shall describe the logic of the program. Logical flow will be presented primarily in the form of macro and micro flowcharts. A narrative presentation or decision tables, when appropriate, will be used to supplement the flowcharts. All flowcharts will be keyed to the higher order flowcharts in the Program Specifications, System/Subsystem Specifications or the Functional Description.

The logical flow shall provide a detailed description of the processing performed by the program. There shall be included for each program function noted in paragraph 2.2 of the Program Specifications a description of the operation of the program. All processes will be described to include algorithmic logic data manipulations and decision processes involved. Conditions being tested for purposes of branching will be explained in detail, as well as methods for identifying error conditions and the resulting actions of the program.

The program macro and micro flowcharts should be included in this section.

SECTION 5. PROGRAM TESTING.

A test must be run before a program is considered to be in an operational status. The following documentation is to be included:

- Description of program test plan
- Description of test data
- Conditions that have been tested
- Results of testing

6. IMPLEMENTATION

Before implementation takes place, management must make certain that information requirements have been correctly defined, that control and audit procedures exist to ensure system integrity, and that performance criteria are documented to measure operational performance against design specifications.

In the implementation phase, system testing, file conversions, and pilot operations are accomplished. While a new system is implemented, user training is completed. The User's Manual is the basis for this training.

The project personnel should prepare the Test Plan, provide assistance and guidance during the implementation, coordinate implementation activities, assure the adequacy of the documentation and controls, prepare fallback procedures in the event of system failures, and make any necessary corrections to the system if deficiencies are uncovered. The new programs are run as a system during system testing to ensure that the program and system interfaces have been properly defined and tested. If an old system exists, parallel runs of the old and new systems may be made to further test the new system. After all test data have been correctly processed, the new system becomes operational.

There are four ways to install the new automated system: (1) install it in a new organization as it is being created, (2) immediately discontinue the old system and switch to the new system, (3) implement the new system in phases, or (4) operate the old and new systems in parallel for some period of time and then discontinue the old system.

The third alternative, implementing a new system in phases, is usually desirable when an organization is upgrading older systems. Systems of major scope that cut across organizational lines and involve numerous organizational components are usually implemented in phases. Implementation may be vertical in the sense of first implementing a production control system, then a marketing information system, and so on. On the other hand, implementation may be horizontal in the sense of meeting the information needs of managers at higher and higher levels of the managerial hierarchy as implementation work progresses.

The fourth alternative calls for the full system or only one part of it to be operated in parallel with an existing system. For example, when parallel operations with the first function indicate accuracy, additional functions can be added to the parallel test. During parallel operations the performance and outputs of the new system are compared with the performance and outputs of the existing system. Although parallel operations may be appropriate in testing some systems, one should be aware of the limitations of such a comparison. As an example, the new system may produce outputs that differ from those of the existing system, thus making direct comparison difficult. Similarly, the inputs to the new system may be very different from those to the existing system, thus requiring precautions in comparing the two systems. Separate controls may have to be maintained and reconciled. The cost of parallel operations is high since it covers duplicate efforts. Because this is so, parallel operations should be scheduled for a limited period of time. During parallel operations the user organization's operating personnel continue to depend upon the existing system. This may impede rapid conversion to the new system. Therefore, parallel operations should be continued only until some predetemined level of performance is achieved.

During the conversion process normal business must continue. The records which are being converted must be available to the operating personnel. One approach is to convert existing records in controllable groups which can be temporarily frozen while conversion takes place. Special programs are generally required to validate records being converted before they are entered into the files for the new system. If existing files do not contain all the data desired for the new system, a decision must be made as to the value of obtaining this data for the new system. If the existing files are highly dynamic, the life of a given record is short. Then it may be unnecessary to convert such files at all.

As work progresses in the implementation phase, three primary documents are produced, namely, the **Test Plan**, the **Test Analysis Report**, and the **User's Manual**. These are discussed in that order.

TEST PLAN

The Test Plan in Illustration **6-1** contains the orderly schedule of events and materials necessary to effectively test and deliver the new system. Step-by-step procedures to accomplish each test of the system are listed. In addition, the stipulations include activities associated with the setup of computer facilities to conduct each test. The parts of the document directed toward management or user personnel should be written in nontechnical language.

The test events are shown in chronological order on a **Test Milestone Chart.** Equipment, software, and personnel necessary for testing are specified. Sample data and work sheets to be utilized during testing are itemized.

System functions to be demonstrated during system testing are described in this plan. As to test methods and constraints, each test is defined in terms of test conditions, test inputs, and test outputs. Methods to be used for the reduction of raw test data into a form suitable for evaluation are defined. The manner and logic of processing from test to test are explained. Criteria for evaluating test results are specified in terms of acceptable tolerances, outputs, and system performance.

TEST PLAN

TABLE OF CONTENTS

ILLUSTRATION 6-1.

SECTION 1. GENERAL

1.1 Purpose of the Test Plan

This paragraph shall describe the purpose of the Test Plan in the following words, modified as appropriate:

The Test Plan for (Project Name) (Project Number) is written to fulfill the following objectives:

- To provide guidance for the management as to the technical effort necessary during the test period.
- To establish a comprehensive test plan and to communicate to the user(s) the nature and extent of the tests necessary to implement the system.
- To coordinate with the user an orderly schedule of events, a specification of equipment and organizational requirements, the methodology of testing, a list of materials to be delivered, and a schedule of user orientation and training.
- To provide a written record of the actual test inputs to exercise system limits and critical capabilities, the instructions to permit

execution of the test by the user staff and operator personnel, and the expected outputs.

1.2 Project References

This paragraph shall provide a brief summary of the references applicable to the history and development of the project. Documentation describing systems or procedures which supplement or provide for interaction with the subject system during the course of normal operation or at any point in the testing shall be specified. Included shall be a listing of at least all prior documentation prepared for this project.

1.3 Deliverable Materials

This paragraph will itemize all materials that will be delivered as part of the system. Included will be the quantity and full identification of the following:

- User's Manual, Operations Manual, and Maintenance Manual.
- Program card decks/listings/card image tapes/ binary tapes.
- Data base card decks/listings/card image tapes.
- Sample listings of system output.

1.4 <u>Statement of Pretest Activity</u>

This paragraph shall provide a description of the testing completed as part of the system development activity. It may refer to an appendix in the form of a listing of the elements in the <u>Program</u> and <u>System/Subsystem Specifications</u> against which the program operation has been explicitly checked. The description should include any significant comments on the operation of the individual programs or subsystems which would affect testing or operation of the system.

SECTION 2. TEST PLAN

2.1 <u>System Description</u>

A brief description or chart showing the data flow of the system shall be included to provide a frame of reference for the description of the tests to be conducted.

2.2 <u>Test Milestone Chart</u>

This paragraph shall provide a chart to depict the activities and events listed below. The chart will be in chronological order with supporting narrative as necessary and will show, for example:

- Overall on-site test period by calendar date and portions of the period assigned to major portions of test.
- Pretest on-site period required for system debugging, orientation, and familiarization.
- Period assigned for the collection of data base values, input values, and other operational data required for system test.
- Period assigned for user orientation and familiarization with system documentation.
- Period assigned for user training, operator training, maintenance and control group training, and orientation briefing for non-ADP personnel.
- Period assigned for compliance with any special test requirements of a particular user.
- Periods assigned for preparation, review, and approval of the <u>Test Analysis Report</u>.

2.3 Environment

This paragraph shall identify the locations at which the testing will be conducted and the participating groups.

2.3.1 Equipment Requirements

This paragraph shall provide a chart or listing to depict the period of usage and quantity required of each item of equipment employed throughout the test period at each location where the system is to be installed. Any test data reduction equipment shall be included.

2.3.2 Software

This paragraph shall list software programs, including systems support and applications programs, and their form (tape,disk,etc.) used during and in support of the testing when they are not a part of the system being tested.

2.3.3 Personnel

This paragraph shall provide a chart or a listing of the number and period of use of personnel with indicated skill types required during the entire test period(s). It will indicate special requirements, such as multishift operation and assignment or the retention of key skills to insure continuity and consistency in extensive test programs. This chart or listing should be related to the Test Milestone Chart.

2.4 Training Plan

This paragraph will describe the number of personnel providing training during the testing and the types of training to be undertaken. This information shall be related to the personnel requirements in paragraph 2.3.3. The training plan shall include user instruction (classroom and computer), operator instruction, maintenance and control group instruction (if applicable) and the orientation of non-ADP personnel.

2.5 Test Materials

This paragraph shall itemize the articles and apparatus associated with the conduct of the test. Examples of these are:

- Data base and its form fully identified.
- Other inputs and their form.
- Test control programs or other special test programs and their form.
- Test work sheets and other forms or instructions prepared to control and expedite the test activity. Their type, layout, and quantity must be fully explained.

Apparatus required during or in support of the test, when it is not normally part of the equipment configuration or is not being delivered as part of the installation effort. Examples of this apparatus are extra peripherals (tape drives, printers, plotters), test message generators, test timing devices, test event records. Such apparatus must be identified by name, type, and quantity required.

SECTION 3. TEST SPECIFICATIONS

3.1 Requirements

This paragraph shall list the individual requirement to be demonstrated by the test as derived from the Specific Performance Requirements given in paragraph 3.1 of the Functional Description.

3.2 System Functions

This paragraph shall provide a detailed list of the system functions which will be exercised during the overall system testing. This list, derived from paragraph 3.2 of the Functional Description, must be ordered in such a way that the functions are related to the requirements given in paragraph 3.1.

3.3 Test/Function Relationships

This paragraph shall provide a list of the tests which, taken as a whole, constitute the overall test activity. It will also provide, as applicable, a Test/Function Matrix Chart summarizing the overall allocation of system functions to the tests.

3.4 Test Methods and Constraints

3.4.1 System Test Conditions

This paragraph shall indicate whether the system test is to be made using the normal system inputs (type, magnitude, or frequency) and data base or whether a special set of exercise inputs and exercise data base is to be used.

3.4.2 System Test Means of Control

This paragraph shall indicate whether the test is to be controlled by:

- Manual means; i.e., manual insertion of necessary inputs and manual control of test sequence.

- Semi-automatic means; i.e., manual insertion of necessary inputs and automatic (test program) control of test sequence.
- Automatic means; i.e., preparation and use of a special test program to provide necessary inputs, conduct tests, monitor, and record test results.

3.4.3 Extent of System Test

This paragraph shall indicate the extent of the testing to be employed. Where total testing is not to be employed, the test requirements will be presented either as a percentage of some well defined total quantity or as a number of samples of discrete operating conditions or values. The rationale for adopting limited testing should be stated.

3.4.4 Data Recording

This paragraph shall indicate data recording requirements including data type recording not normally recovered from system operation.

3.4.5 System Test Constraints

This paragraph shall indicate the anticipated limitations imposed on the test due to system or test conditions, such as limitations on timing, interfaces, equipment, personnel, and data base.

SECTION 4. TEST DESCRIPTIONS

4.1 Test Progression

In cases of progressive or cumulative tests, an explanation shall be included concerning the manner in which progression is made from one test to another so that the cycle of activity for each test is completely accomplished.

4.2 Test (Identify) Description

A description of each test to be conducted shall be included as paragraphs 4.2 through 4.n. The following are typical of the information that should be provided for each test.

4.2.1 Test Inputs

This paragraph shall list the input or inputs to the test with their associated data characteristics. Data characteristics include:

- Type of input (data elements, command

instructions).

- Transfer (data rate, volume, period).

4.2.2 Test Outputs

This paragraph shall list the output or outputs from the test with their associated data characteristics. Data characteristics include:

- Type of output (data presentation, status indication).
- Transfer (data rate, volume, period).

4.2.3 Test Conditions

This paragraph shall provide a statement of conditions which exist within the test or as part of the input or output to the test. Conditions include:

- Setting of controlling parameters for the test (minimum, maximums, thresholds).
- Enabling conditions for receipt or output of data.
- Priority conditions for processing data (function priorities, system mode priorities).

4.2.4 System Conditions

This paragraph shall provide a statement of

conditions which exist within the system prior to test. Conditions include:

- Availability of file data types and elements.
- Availability of data, control, and status messages from interacting functions not under test.
- Mode of system operation (normal, emergency).

4.2.5 Test Control

4.2.5.1 Input Data

This paragraph will describe the manner in which input data is controlled in order to:

- Test the system with a minimum number of data types and values.
- Exercise the system with a range of valid data types and values which test for overload, saturation, and other "worst case" effects.
- Exercise the system with invalid data types and values which test for rejection of irregular inputs.

4.2.5.2 Input Commands

This paragraph shall describe the manner in which input commands are used to control:

- Initialization of test.
- Halt or interrupt of test.
- Repeat of unsuccessful or incomplete test.
- Alternate modes of operation as required by test.
- Termination of test.

4.2.5.3 Output Data

This paragraph shall describe the manner in which output data is controlled in order to:

- Detect occurrence of output data for indication of test completion.
- Record or identify permanent location of output data for indication of test performance.
- Evaluate output as a basis for continuation of test sequence.

- Evaluate test output against required output to assess the performance of the test.

4.2.5.4 Output Notification

This paragraph shall describe the manner in which output notifications (messages output by the system concerning status or limitations on internal performance) are controlled in order to:

- Indicate readiness for test.
- Provide indications of irregularities in input test data or test data base.
- Provide indications of irregularities in internal operations on test data.
- Provide indications on the control, status, and results of the test.

SECTION 5. TEST PROCEDURES

This section shall contain the step-by-step procedures to accomplish each test of the system. Each step shall be assigned a test step number and this number, along with critical test data and test procedure information, shall be tabulated onto a test procedure form for test control and the recording of test results.

5.1 Test Setup

If not stated elsewhere or by standard operating procedures, this paragraph shall itemize the activities associated with setup of the computer facilities to conduct the test, including all routine machine activities from "power on" through "console setup" to "card/tape read in." Included shall be the distribution of test documents, worksheets, and other forms.

5.2 Test Initialization

This paragraph shall itemize in test sequence order the activities associated with establishing the conditions of the first test starting with the equipment in the setup condition. Initialization may include such functions as:

- Read-out of control function locations and critical

data from indicators and storage locations for reference purposes.

- Queuing of data input values for first test.
- Queuing of test support programs.
- Coordination of personnel actions associated with test.

5.3 Test Steps

This paragraph shall itemize the test(s) into test steps in test sequence order. It shall also include special operations, such as:

- Visual inspection of test conditions.
- Data dumps.
- Instructions for data recording.
- Modifications of data base.
- Interim evaluation of test results.

5.4 Test Termination

This paragraph shall itemize in test sequence order

the activities associated with termination of the test, such as:

- Read-out of critical data from indicators for reference purposes.
- Termination of operation of time sensitive test support programs and test apparatus.
- Collection of system and operator records of test results.

SECTION 6. TEST EVALUATION

6.1 Test Data Criteria

This paragraph shall describe the rules by which test results will be evaluated, for example:

- Tolerances - range over which a data value can vary and still be considered acceptable.
- Samples - the minimum number of combinations or alternatives of input conditions and output conditions that can be exercised to constitute an acceptable test of the parameters involved.

- Counts - the maximum number of interrupts, halts, or other system breaks which may occur due to non-test conditions.

6.2 Test Data Reduction

This paragraph shall describe the technique to be used for manipulation of the raw test data into a form suitable for evaluation. The available techniques would include:

- Manual; i.e., manual collection and collation of system test outputs into test sequence order followed by visual inspection of the results.
- Semi-automatic; i.e., automatic inspection of test results as obtained by data recording means using a test data reduction program followed by manual (visual) inspection of selected test results which do not lend themselves to complete reduction by automatic means.
- Automatic; i.e., automatic inspection of test results specially recorded for manipulation by the test data reduction program. Test results, as recorded, include all items of test significance. The test data reduction program contains an image of correct

data output for an item-by-item comparison of data and provides a summary of an evaluated test as output. The outputs produced from these data reduction techniques should be described and, if appropriate, illustrated. Limitations in data reduction capabilities should be stated and the effect of these limitations on the testing of the system.

TEST ANALYSIS REPORT

The Test Analysis Report, prepared in nontechnical language, describes the status of the computer system after testing and provides a presentation of deficiencies for review by the user organization's management and operations personnel. Illustration **6-2** shows the contents of this report.

The tests being documented are related to the testing sequence described in the Test Plan. Each test is separately identified, and the objectives of each test are defined. Descriptions are given for each function that was tested and for the demonstrated capability of the system to perform the function. The manner in which the test environment may differ from the operational system environment is assessed.

The system is measured against the performance specifications in the Test Plan. In the definition of the impact of each observed deficiency on the performance of the system, the organization responsible for correcting the deficiency is included. Finally, definitions are included for each improvement or refinement that can be made to the system and for the capability each refinement would add to the system.

Prior to the acceptance test, the project team can follow a top-down approach and effectively perform many integration tests for each of the subsystems and for the entire system. The conditions for testing should be as close to actual operating conditions as possible. Personnel from the user organization should be involved to prepare the data used for testing. They can also perform all operational functions.

Sufficient test data to test all automated processes in the system should be generated. The testing should demonstrate that data generated by one process can be used effectively by subsequent processes for which the data is intended.

As part of the preparation for these tests, a description of the criteria upon which the subsystems will be evaluated and accepted should be documented. These criteria will establish standards by which the system performance may be measured to assure that original requirements have been met. The next phase involves the process of placing the entire system into operation. This includes the initial creation of files and tables for each subsystem, subsystem conversion, and running the entire system to create the desired outputs for each subsystem.

TEST ANALYSIS REPORT

TABLE OF CONTENTS

ILLUSTRATION 6-2.

SECTION 1. GENERAL

1.1 Purpose of Test Analysis Report

This paragraph shall describe the purpose of the Test Analysis Report in the following words or appropriate modifications thereto:

The Test Analysis Report for (Project Name) (Project Number) is written to fulfill the following objectives:

- To document the results of the implementation test.
- To provide a basis for allocating responsibility for deficiency correction and follow-up.
- To provide a basis for the preparation of the statement of project completion.
- To establish user confidence in the operation of the system.

1.2 Project References

This paragraph shall provide a brief summary of the

project objectives and identify the project sponsor and user. Also, provided shall be a list of applicable documents by author or source, reference number, and title. This paragraph will include the following, when applicable:

- Functional Description
- User's Manual
- Operations Manual
- Maintenance Manual
- Test Plan

SECTION 2. TEST ANALYSIS

The tests described in this section must be related to those presented in the Test Plan.

2.1 Test (Identify)

Each test shall be separately identified in paragraphs 2.1 through 2.n.

2.1.1 Data Performance

This paragraph shall compare the I/O performance

of the test with the I/O capabilities as described in the User's Manual and the Test Plan.

2.1.2 Parameter Performance

This paragraph shall compare the parameter performance of the test with the parameter performance described in the User's Manual, Operations Manual, and the Test Plan.

2.2 Test (Identify)

This paragraph shall present information on the second test in a manner similar to that used in paragraph 2.1.

SECTION 3. SYSTEM FUNCTION ANALYSIS

3.1 System Function (Identify)

Each system function shall be separately described in paragraphs 3.1 through 3.n corresponding to the functions presented in paragraph 3.2 of the Test Plan.

3.1.1 Function Performance

This paragraph shall describe the capability as it has been demonstrated in one or more system tests. It shall also assess the manner in which the test environment may be different from the operational environment and the effect of this difference on the capability.

3.1.2 Performance Limits

This paragraph shall describe the range of data and parameter values tested. It shall also identify any deficiencies, limitations, or constraints inherent in the system detected during the testing process.

3.2 System Function (Identify)

This paragraph shall present information on the second system function in a manner similar to that used in paragraph 3.1.

SECTION 4. SUMMARY AND CONCLUSIONS

4.1 Demonstrated Capability

This paragraph shall provide a general statement of the capability of the system as demonstrated by the test, compared with the performance requirements contained in the Functional Description of the system. An individual discussion of conformance with specific requirements should be included on complex systems.

4.2 System Deficiencies

As required by the results of the testing, an individual statement will be provided for each deficiency in system operations, as measured against the Test Plan. Accompanying each deficiency will be a discussion of the impact on system performance, if the deficiency is retained and the impact on the system design, if the deficiency is corrected, along with the assignment of organizational responsibility for the correction.

4.3 System Refinements

An itemization of improvements which can be realized in system design or operation, as determined during the test period. Accompanying each improvement will be a discussion of the added capability it provides the system and the impact on the system design.

USER'S MANUAL

The primary purpose of the User's Manual is to serve the needs of the user organization. The manual shows the relationships between the functions performed by the system and the organization's departments that are sources of input to the system as well as those that are recipients of output from it. Furthermore, it provides management with a summary of the capabilities of the existing system and describes capabilities that can be added to the system.

The manual contains instructional material for entering data into the system and for properly using output from the system. For example, the manual specifies the user's responsibilities for batching input data, establishing document controls, meeting data preparation deadlines, and validating the receipt and accuracy of output reports.

Sections 1 and 2 of the User's Manual (see Illustration **6-3**) present general and specific information on the application and are directed toward general management and user personnel who do not need detailed technical information concerning system implementation or operation. Sections 3 and 4 are more detailed and discuss system inputs, system messages, and system outputs. Instructions for the operation of specific consoles or terminals should be included in appropriate appendices.

The installation of a complex computer system requires the extensive training of the user personnel. A lack of adequate training at all levels of management will reduce the effectiveness of the system. Executives must fully comprehend the system's goals and procedures if their support is to be obtained. Similarly, middle management must also understand the system in sufficient depth to supervise its operation. The details of system processing must be learned by the user organization's operations personnel.

One of the limiting factors currently preventing computer users from realizing the full potential of the computer is the scarcity of qualified systems personnel. It may be necessary for a user organization to obtain needed expertise by training new and existing personnel for operating a new system. Most user organizations will need to develop some suitable approach to ensure that their experienced and new employees are trained to perform their new functions effectively.

Prior to designing a training program for the implementation of the new system, its objectives should be clearly defined. A fundamental objective is to thoroughly train the user personnel in the operation of the new system. Quality training will minimize failures in system performance due to errors by the user organization's personnel. Those who are responsible for input to the computer -- the clerks, administrators, secretaries, and supervisors in the user organization's departments -- often receive inadequate preparation. Short seminars in system operation, preferably with system personnel in attendance, are usually mandatory for successful system implementation.

USER'S MANUAL

TABLE OF CONTENTS

ILLUSTRATION 6-3.

SECTION 1. GENERAL DESCRIPTION

1.1 Purpose of the User's Manual

This paragraph shall describe the purpose of the User's Manual in the following words, modified when appropriate:

> The objective of the User's Manual for (Project Name) (Project Number) is to provide the user's non-ADP personnel with the information necessary to effectively use the system.

1.2 Project References

This paragraph shall provide a brief summary of the references applicable to the history and development of the project. A list of applicable documents shall be included. At least the following shall be specified by author or source, reference number, and title.

- Project request.
- Previously published documentation on the project.
- Documentation concerning related projects.
- Standards or reference documentation.

SECTION 2. SYSTEM SUMMARY

2.1 System Application

The uses of the application in supporting the activities of the user's staff shall be generally stated and explained. The description shall include:

- The purpose, reason, or rationale of the system.
- Capabilities and operating improvements provided by the system.
- Additional features, characteristics, and advantages considered appropriate to furnish a clear description of the system and the benefits derived from it.
- Functions performed by the system.

2.2 System Operation

This paragraph will show the relationships of the functions performed by the system with the organizations that are sources of input to the system and those that are recipients of output from it. Included will be charts and a brief narrative description of system inputs and outputs.

2.3 System Configuration

A brief narrative description of the equipment used by the system shall be given. It may include the type of computer and input and output devices.

2.4 System Organization

The objective of this paragraph shall be to present a general overview of the organization of the system. The presentation shall show, as appropriate, the logical parts of the system and a brief description of their role in the operation of the system.

2.5 Performance

This paragraph shall present a brief description of the overall performance capabilities of the system, including how it meets the information requirements of the user. Performance measures and information of interest are represented by the following examples:

- Input - types, volumes, rate of inputs accepted.
- Output - types, volume, accuracy, rate of outputs that the system can produce.

- Response time - include qualifications that affect response time in processing operational reports, such as listing a tape, compiling an object program. Type and volume of input and equipment configuration are examples of items that may influence running time and response time.
- Limitations - for example, maximum size per unit of input, format constraints, restrictions on which data files may be queried.
- Error rate - capabilities for detecting various legal and logical errors and the means provided for error correction.
- Processing time - show typical processing times.
- Flexibility - note provisions allowing extension of the usage of the system.
- Reliability - note system provisions that support, for example, alternate processing or a switch-over capability.

2.6 Data Base

The data files that are referenced, supported, or

kept current by the system shall be described. These files shall be identified in operational or functional terms rather than by program designations. The brief description should include the type of data in the file and the usage made of it.

2.7 General Description of Inputs, Processing, Outputs

This paragraph shall present a general narrative description of the inputs, the flow of data through the processing cycle, and the resultant outputs.

- Inputs - In describing the inputs, consideration shall be given to the following:
  - Purpose of input - explain why the input is made to the program system and note conditions or events requiring its submission.
  - Content of input - describe what the input contains in the way of operational, control, or reference data.
  - Associated inputs - describe any other inputs required by the system in addition to the direct input.

- Origin of inputs - identify the source or preparer of the input.
- Data files - identify in general or functional terms the data files associated with the input.
- Other - include additional remarks of general information.

- Processing - In this paragraph, the relationship of the input to the output should be described with a general description of the flow of data through the processing cycle.
- Outputs - In describing the outputs, consideration should be given to the following:
  - Output - list the outputs produced by the system showing their relationship to the inputs.
  - Purpose of output - explain the reason for the output and note conditions or events that require its generation by the system.
  - Content of output - describe in general terms the information provided by the output.
  - Associated outputs - reference other system outputs that complement the information in this output.

- Distribution of outputs - note the recipients in the organization who receive this output.
- Other - describe additional items of general information.

SECTION 3. SYSTEM OPERATIONS

Section 3 of the _User's Manual_ shall provide the details necessary to prepare user inputs to the system. The scope, quality, and logical arrangement of the information shall enable the user personnel to prepare inputs correctly and expeditiously. In addition, this section will explain in detail the characteristics and meaning of the information the program system produces as outputs.

3.1 _Staff Input Requirements_

The requirements to be observed in preparing entries to the system shall be delineated in this paragraph for each different type or class of input. Typical considerations are the following:

- Cause of input - note what operational conditions require the submission of the input (e.g., normal status report, need to enter parameters in a source program, need to update data, the desire to obtain particular data, the need to respond to a particular display).

- Time of input - specify when the input must be prepared (e.g., periodically, randomly as a function of an operational situation).
- Origin of input - identify the user personnel authorized to generate the input.
- Medium of input - note the medium used to enter the input (e.g., keyboard, punched card, magnetic or paper tape).
- Associated inputs - reference any related inputs that are required to be entered at the same time as this input.
- Other - note any other applicable information, such as other recipients of the inputs, priority handling, variations on the basic input format using code or key indicators, limitations on what files may be interrogated by a particular type of input.

3.2 Composition Rules

This paragraph shall provide a description of the language and the grammatical rules and conventions that must be observed in order to prepare input that can be accepted by the program system. The rules of syntax and usage of punctuation will be explained. Items for considerations may include the following:

- Input length - e.g., 100 characters maximum.
- Line length - e.g., 30 characters maximum.
- Format - e.g., all input items must be left justified.
- Labeling - i.e., usage of tags or identifiers to denote major data sets to the system.
- Sequencing - i.e., the order and placement of items in the input.
- Punctuation - i.e., spacing and use of symbols to denote start and end of input, of lines, of data groups.
- Combination - i.e., rules forbidding use of particular character or parameter sets in an input.

3.3 Vocabulary

This paragraph shall explain the legal character combinations or codes that can be used to identify or compose input items. Included may be codes for data file or call-up parameters, inventory items, statements, or operations.

3.4 Input Formats

The layout form(s) used in the initial preparation of system inputs shall be illustrated and the information which may be entered on the various sections and lines explained. The explanation of each entry provision shall be keyed to the sample form illustrated. Also note the need for any "job submission" or "request for computer services" form that represents the formal interface between user and computer control personnel.

3.5 Sample Inputs

Each class or type of input acceptable to the system shall be illustrated. An introduction will be given as to what the sample represents. A complete explanation shall follow, describing the significance of the subsections of the sample input. Included in the explanation may be information on the following types of inputs:

- Control or header - containing entries that denote the input class or type, date/time, origin, instruction codes to the system.
- Text - containing the subsections of the input representing data for operational files, request parameters for an information retrieval program.
- Trailer - containing control data denoting the end of input and any additional control data.
- Omissions - indicate those classes or types of inputs that may be omitted at the option of the user or because of particular circumstances concerning the input.
- Repeats - indicate those subsections of the input that may be repeated up to a specified maximum number of entries.

3.6 Output Requirements

The requirements relevant to each class of output

shall be described. Representative information that may be included for each class of output is:

- Purpose - the reason(s) why the output is generated; e.g., the desire to obtain particular data, due to the existence of an "exception" situation.
- Time - whether the output is randomly or periodically produced. If produced periodically, the period must be specified.
- Modes - any modifications or variations of the basic output that are available.
- Medium - the physical form of the output, such as printout, CRT, tape, cards.
- Location - where the output is required to appear, such as in the computer area or remotely at a particular terminal location.
- Other - any additional requirements for this output, such as priority handling.

3.7 Output Formats

The layout in which each class or type of system output is presented shall be explained in detail. Explanations shall be keyed to particular parts of the format illustrated. Appropriate information that may be provided includes the following:

- Header - the title, identification, time, number of output parts, and similar basic control data that may be contained in the header or control segment of the output shall be described.

- Body - the information that may appear in the body or text of the output must be explained. Described should be the significance of fixed data, such as columnar headings in tabular display types of output. The existence of sub-sets or sections in the output format (e.g., part A, part B) should be noted. In card/tape output, the position or column locations allocated to specific output information should be described.

- Trailer - the control or reference information that may be appended to the body of information presented shall be discussed.

Additional characteristics concerning the make-up of outputs may include information such as the meanings of special symbols.

3.8 Sample Outputs

Illustrations of the types of output obtainable from the system shall be given for each different class of output. The function or purpose of the sample output shall be explained. A detailed description will be provided for each sample including the following:

- Definition - the meaning and use of each information variable.
- Source - item extracted from a specific input, from a data base file, calculated by system.
- Characteristics - concerning omissibility of the item under certain conditions of the output generation, range of values, unit of measure.

SECTION 4. FILE QUERY PROCEDURES

This section shall be prepared for those applications with a file query retrieval capability. The instructions necessary for recognition, preparation, and processing of a query applicable to the data base shall be cited in detail. The descriptive techniques illustrated in paragraphs 4.1, 4.2 and 4.3 shall be utilized as applicable.

4.1 System Query Capabilities

This paragraph shall illustrate in tabular form the pre-programmed query capabilities provided by the system with a cross-reference to a query card format or query statement.

4.2 Data Base Format

This paragraph shall illustrate the data base format and content. If applicable, data which are not subject to queries and data, even though not specifically requested, which must be extracted for all queries shall be indicated. In addition to item names, appropriate mnemonics for the item names should be given as necessary for clarity.

4.3 Query Preparation

Instructions shall be provided for the preparation of any necessary query title, request, and parameter input. The details of query input preparation in the context of each specific data base and system retrieval capability shall be repeated as necessary in the form of positive instructions. In cases when the retrieval capability is part of a support system and query input formats are not needed, the specific query statement required shall be listed.

4.4 Control Instructions

Instructions shall be provided for the control of the sequencing of runs and of the program necessary to extract the response to the query request from the data base. These instructions shall include the requirements for, and the preparation of, control cards which may be required by the system or application programs. If extensive information concerning control card preparation is contained in support system documentation, this documentation may be referenced.

7. OPERATION

After the system has been fully tested, and user personnel have been trained, and conversion has been completed, the system becomes operational. At the conclusion of implementation, the user staff and computer operations staff accept responsibility for the continuing operation of the new computer application. Their acceptance of the new system requires a formal review of the system documentation, system testing, and user training.

An **Operations Manual** details system operating procedures to the computer operations staff. Requirements for system maintenance are specified in the **Maintenance Manual.** The operational system should be analyzed relative to the specifications contained in the Functional Description and System Design Report. This analysis is summarized in the **Evaluation Report.**

OPERATIONS MANUAL

An Operations Manual provides operations personnel with a detailed description of the system and with the operating procedures necessary to operate the application. This manual contains setup procedures, work schedules, control procedures, data retention schedules, and similar control and procedural information. Illustration **7-1** shows the contents of this manual.

A chart shows the data flow and operations, and a narrative explains how various operations are interrelated relative to input data and output information. Each set of operations required on a daily, weekly, or monthly basis is presented. All necessary control and scheduling procedures are listed for each operation. The manual also defines responsibilities for the administration, security, and control of the operational system. Each control form is illustrated, and the function of each form is described. Data retention schedules are specified and conform to the policies of the organization. With on-line systems, the description of system operational controls will relate to capabilities of the operating system software.

OPERATIONS MANUAL

TABLE OF CONTENTS

ILLUSTRATION 7-1.

SECTION 1. GENERAL DESCRIPTION

1.1 Purpose of Operations Manual

This paragraph shall describe the purpose of the Operations Manual in the following words or appropriate modifications thereto:

> The objective of this Operations Manual (Project Name) (Project Number) is to provide computer control and computer operator personnel with a detailed operational description of the system and its associated environment with which they will be concerned during the performance of their duties.

1.2 System Application

A brief description of the system shall include its purpose and uses and all reference related User and Maintenance Manuals.

1.3 System Operation

This paragraph shall describe the operation of the system by use of a chart showing the data flow and data processing operations, including how the various operations are interrelated relative to input data and output information. If sets of runs are grouped by periods of time cycles, then each set of integrated operations required on a daily, weekly, or monthly basis will be presented. The interrelationships among the system tasks with respect to timing and input/output data are of primary importance to control personnel.

1.4 Program Inventory

This paragraph shall provide an inventory in tabular form of the various system operations. Each shall be identified by title, number, and mnemonic reference. The use and approximate timing requirements by equipment (including keypunching) of each operation will also be given.

SECTION 2. SYSTEM CONTROL

Section 2 of the Operations Manual shall present information on how the operations and environment associated with the system are controlled so that scheduling of operations, assignment of equipments, and the management of input data, output data, and other output information may proceed in an orderly and productive manner. With on-line systems, some of the description of system operational control will be related to the capability of the supervisory program which functions as a real-time controller of the operations and environment.

2.1 Control Requirements

This paragraph shall present clear and concise instructions for control personnel, who are responsible for the overall administration, security, and control of the operation of the computer programs. Where applicable, reference should be made to the flowchart referenced in paragraph 1.3. The following items are representative of control considerations which may be applicable:

- Processing cycles (continuously, daily, weekly, monthly).
- Receipt time and identity of input (data, parameters).
- Coordination and control (including security) of input, library, and output material.
- Instructions for the preparation of the data and required control cards.
- Composition of instruction forms.

- Preliminary EAM processing instructions (major EAM operations are to be presented in detail in Section 3).
- Quality control techniques.
- Disposition of output.
- Disposition of input after processing.

2.2 Control Forms

This paragraph shall present illustrations of the applicable forms that support the various system control requirements. If a form is to be designed, each form shall be identified by name/title, form number, and functional use in the scheme of control. The significance of each entry provision in the form shall be explained.

- Request for Computer Processing - This form should be designed to facilitate rapid recognition of the requirements of the user and to interface with control instructions.
- Graphic Processing Chart - The Graphic Processing Chart is essentially a macro flowchart, modified to serve as a request document for requesting and controlling production processing operations. With the concurrence of the data administrator of the

user, Graphic Processing Charts may be prepared for each system or each major logical portion of the system.

2.3 Phasing

This paragraph shall provide a schedule of acceptable phasing of the system into a logical series of operations. A system run may be phased to permit manual or semi-automatic checking of intermediate results, to provide the user with intermediate results for other purposes, or to permit a logical break if higher priority jobs are submitted. An example of the minimum division for most systems would be edit, file update, and report preparation.

2.4 Data Retention Schedules

- Data retention schedules shall be developed in accordance with the requirements of the data base administrator. Due consideration must be given to the schedule so that it will reflect realistic retention periods.

- Included must be considerations of the various media on which the data is recorded, such as paper tape. disks, and magnetic tapes. The temporary retention of data during processing cycles should be considered to allow time for the verification of output prior to the destruction of the original data, to provide back-up capabilities.

Basic information required is as follows:

- Project Number
- Subsystem number
- Run number generated
- Tape name
- Retention schedule to include:
    - Retention duration
    - Release data (if applicable)
    - Replacement instructions

SECTION 3. OPERATING PROCEDURES

Section 3 of the Operations Manual shall present the procedures and materials required to perform each of the individual operations for both computer and EAM equipments. The presentation of procedural actions and responses required of the operator with regard to inputs, machine indications, and outputs expected shall be made in a logical manner and shall follow the sequence normally required in performing the run. In addition, procedures covering the occurrence of abnormal or unexpected operations shall be provided.

3.1 EDP Tasks

All necessary procedures and input/output information shall be presented for each computer run or operation of the subject system, including any pre-storing or post-processing. The scope and content of the information presented will enable control personnel to specify in detail the materials and procedures required for the operator(s) to perform the computer run or job. Representative of the information required for each computer run is that included in the following paragraphs.

3.1.1 Equipment Configuration

All equipment required to perform the tasks shall be listed and identified. Significant alternative configurations should be shown with any necessary interconnections.

3.1.2 Input Materials

In general, the physical form of the input will be punched cards, paper or magnetic tape, or keyboard messages. Functionally, the inputs will represent a program to be loaded, input data (reference or current transactions), or both. Provision shall be made for indicating the version of the program and data to be used. Representative of the detailed information needed for input materials is the following:

- Control/administrative forms authorizing the run.
- Input data forms or decks - e.g., name, general content, sequence.
- Instruction forms specifying what is to be done to the input.
- Sources of input materials - e.g., control supervisor, operator of a prior run.
- Disposition of input materials - e.g., return to control supervisor, pass to operator of a succeeding run.

3.1.3 Output Expected

In general, the outputs can be produced as punched cards, paper or magnetic tape, hard copy printouts, or CRT displays that contain the information desired from the program run. The following are representative of the detailed information needed concerning expected outputs:

- Specify the output(s) expected.
- Note any checks or verifications that may be required.
- Specify the disposition of the output; e.g., forward to control supervisor, forward to operator of a succeeding run. Note also any requirements for binding, deleaving, packaging, labeling, and the like.

3.1.4 Procedures

These procedures should be limited to those which are unique to the particular system being run and not those which must be followed for all runs made on the hardware system.

3.1.4.1 Setup

- These procedures shall itemize the logical sequence of operator actions in selecting and initializing the specified peripherals and the central processor console so that the programs associated with the run may be loaded and readied for operation. On-line runs may have a control program assisting in setup procedures and communicating instructions to the operator via the control console. Use of preprinted forms or multiple ply paper for the printer should be noted.

- Samples of completed run sheets will be included. The development of individual run sheets will be coordinated with the user in order to insure compatibility with existing user requirements.

3.1.4.2 Operation

- These procedures shall itemize the logical sequence of operator actions in loading the input data (dynamic and reference) for entry into the processor and initiating the run at the console. Attention shall be given to noting the correct sequence or order of the reading of data (e.g., control cards for date, job number, file ID, followed by data sets and end-of-input cards). An illustration of the card deck sequence for each run along with a card image listing should be included.

- Input keyboard messages for on-line operations will provide similar system direction by virtue of their header information. Included in this section shall be applicable information on data processor-operator communications that can occur during the run. Specifically, tabulations shall be presented on:
    - Error messages.
    - Program normal halts.
    - Program abnormal halts.

  The tabulation shall identify the output, its cause, its medium (console typewriter, card punch, printer, or console register display), the response or action required of the operator and any feedback or response from the processor as a result of the action. Examples will be given of the formats of these inputs and outputs.

3.1.4.3 Termination

These procedures shall inform the operator of the sequence of actions that must be followed to return the processor and the peripherals to their standby conditions when setup procedures have been utilized that are other than standard.

3.2 EAM Tasks

EAM tasks unique to the particular system will be presented. EAM tasks which are routine with most systems, such as key punching and verifying, will be excluded unless necessary for clarity. The basic sequence of setup-operate-terminate shall be followed in presenting the EAM run procedures. Representative of the items for which detailed information is required for each EAM run are those included in the following paragraphs.

3.2.1 Equipment Configuration

The EAM units required to perform each task shall be listed and identified.

3.2.2 Input Materials

The checklist of items listed in paragraph 3.1.2 is applicable to EAM runs.

3.2.3 Outputs Expected

The checklist of items under paragraph 3.1.3 is applicable to EAM runs.

3.2.4 Procedures

Step-by-step requirements shall be itemized for actions, indications, and responses for the operator in setting up, operating, and terminating the run (setting of switches, insertion of program boards). Operator actions shall be included, where appropriate, in response to an aborted run e.g., restart, notify supervisor, or perform EAM maintenance. A flow diagram of EAM tasks shall be included.

SECTION 4. NON-ROUTINE OPERATIONS

The purpose of Section 4 of the Operations Manual shall be to provide control information and operator procedures to cover emergency or non-routine computer operations. Representative of the situations that may be covered in the paragraphs of this section are the following:

- Recovery from a failure condition
- Switchover to a redundant system or to a standby system.
- Procedures for turnover to maintenance programmers for system testing, modification or debugging.
- Normal and priority restart procedures.

MAINTENANCE MANUAL

The Maintenance Manual describes the maintenance requirements for the computer application. The manual contains the details and characteristics of each program and subroutine that would be of value to a maintenance programmer in understanding the programs and their relationships. The manual identifies specific procedures that the programmer should follow to properly maintain the system (see Illustration **7-2**).

After a system becomes operational, it must be maintained. Changes in an organization's policies and procedures, changes in work flow, changes in equipment, or programming improvements can all create a need to modify an operational computer application. Good maintenance documentation simplifies the implementation and testing of changes to a system. After a change has been implemented, the modified system should not be utilized for production until the system has been fully tested. The system documentation must also be updated to reflect the system modification.

MAINTENANCE MANUAL

TABLE OF CONTENTS

ILLUSTRATION 7-2.

SECTION 1. GENERAL DESCRIPTION

1.1 Purpose of the Maintenance Manual

This paragraph shall describe the purpose of the Maintenance Manual in the following words or appropriate modifications thereto:

> The objective for writing this Maintenance Manual for (Project Name) (Project Number) is to provide the maintenance programmer personnel with the information necessary to effectively maintain the system.

1.2 System Application

The purpose of the system and the functions it performs shall be explained in general non-ADP terms. A particular application system, for example, might serve to control economic activities by accepting specific inputs, extracting items of data, and deriving other items of data in order to produce information about a specific trend and for summary reports. These functions shall be related to paragraphs 3.1, Specific Performance Requirements, and 3.2, System Functions, of the FD (Functional Description).

1.3 Equipment Environment

This paragraph shall discuss the equipment configuration and its general characteristics as they apply to the system.

1.4 Program Environment

This paragraph will present the interactions of the application programs with any controlling system, support system, and any other application program. If the program utilizes a general system support capability as an integral part of its overall design, this paragraph should state what these systems are and whether or not a basic understanding of them is a prerequisite for effectively utilizing the program being described.

1.5 Conventions

This paragraph will explain all rules, schemes, and conventions that have been used within the system. Information of this nature would include the following items:

- Design of mnemonic identifiers and their application to the tagging or labeling of programs, subroutines, records, data fields, storage areas.
- Procedures and standards for flowcharts, listings, serialization of cards, abbreviations used in statements and remarks, and symbols appearing in charts and listings.
- The appropriate standards, fully identified, may be referenced in lieu of a detailed outline of conventions.

SECTION 2. SYSTEM DESCRIPTION

The purpose of Section 2 is to show the structure, operation, and composition of the system as a program or a set of interrelated programs.

2.1 General Description

This paragraph will provide a comprehensive description of the system, subsystem, jobs in terms of their overall functions. This description will be accompanied by a chart showing the interrelationships of the major components of the system.

2.2 Detailed Description

The purpose of this paragraph is to supply details and characteristics of each program and subroutine that would be of value to a maintenance programmer in understanding the program and its relationship to other programs. This paragraph will initially contain a list of all programs to be discussed, followed by a narrative description of each program and its respective subroutines under separate paragraphs starting with 2.2.1 through 2.2.n. Information to be included in the narrative description is represented by the following items:

- Program title or tag (including a designation of the version number of the program).
- Description of program functions.
- Storage - Specify the amount of storage required to use the program and the broad parameters of the storage locations needed.
- Data file records used by the program during operation.

- Branching conditions provided in the program.
- Entry requirements concerning the initiation of the program.
- Input data type and location(s) used by the program when its operation begins.
- Exit requirements concerning termination of the operation of the program.
- Communications or linkage to the next logical program (operational, control).
- Output data type and location(s) produced by the program for use by related processing segments of the system.
- Response to errors detected during the input-processing-output operations of the program.
- Restrictions that have been designed into the system with respect to the operation of this program, or any limitations on the use of the program.
- Permanency - Note whether the program is a normal link in the cycle of programs to be run or will be used only under certain circumstances.

- Associated programs - Identify the programs which can access this program.
- Major operations - The major operations of each program will also be described. The description shall be referenced to flowchart(s) which may be included in an appendix. This flowchart will show the general logical flow of operations, such as read an input, access a data record, which would be represented by segments or subprograms within the program. Reference may be made to included flowcharts that present each major operation in more detail.

SECTION 3. INPUT/OUTPUT DESCRIPTIONS

The purpose of Section 3 of the manual shall be to provide information on the structure and composition of the system data.

3.1 General Description

This paragraph shall provide a general presentation of the inputs and outputs in regard to scope and the variety of information available in support of the system and maintained by the system.

3.2 Characteristics, Organization, and Detailed Description of System Data

3.2.1 General Characteristics

Information in this paragraph shall include a complete description of the nature and content of each of the input/output components that make up the system data. The following are examples of this type of information:

- Identification - Name and mnemonic reference of the component (e.g., data base). List the programs utilizing the component.
- Function - Explain the use of the component in the system.
- Content - Describe the kind of data it holds. This may be operational data (input data, output information, reference data), internal data such as results of intermediate processing, or director information (routing/linkage tables)

- that enables a program to locate other records or to communicate with other programs.
- Permanency - Note whether the component contains static data that a program can reference but may not change or dynamic data that can be changed or updated during system operation. Indicate whether the change is periodic or random as a function of input data.
- Storage - Specify the location(s) in which the data base information is held (e.g., tape, disk, internal storage) and the amount of storage required.
- Associated programs - Identify the programs which can access this component during their operation. Indicate if the program only reads data or may also write new data into the record.
- Restrictions - Explain any limitations on the use of this component by the programs in the system.

3.2.2 <u>Organization and Detailed Description</u>

This paragraph will serve to define the internal structure of each input/output component. An example of each will be shown and its composition, such as records and tables, will be explained. The following items indicate the type of information desired:

- Layout - Show the structure of the subject record.
- Sections - Note whether the physical record is a logical record or one of several that constitute the complete logical record. Identify the record parts, such as header or control segments and the body of the record.
- Fields - Identify each field of data provided in the record structure and explain its purpose.
- Tags/labels - Indicate the tag or label assigned to reference each field of data.
- Size - Indicate the length and number of bits/characters that make up each data field.

- Range - Indicate the range of acceptable values for the field entry, if a numeric.
- Expansion - Note provisions, if any, for adding additional data fields to the record.

3.3 Tables

The tables within each program of the system shall be explained and described. Reference may be made to the program listing but this paragraph should provide the information necessary to understand the use of the tables specified in that listing. Such information includes:

- Table tag, label or symbolic name.
- Full name or purpose of the table.
- Program that uses this table.
- Logical divisions with the table (internal table blocks or parts - not entries).
- Basic table structure (fixed or variable length, fixed or variable entry structure).
- Table layout (a graphic presentation should be used). Included in supporting description should

be table control information, details of the structure of each type of entry, unique or significant characteristics of the use of the table.

3.4 Items

As used in this paragraph, the word "item" refers to a specific category of detailed information that has a defined position within a table and that is coded for direct and immediate manipulation by a program. This information may be presented within the description of the table that contains the item. Of primary importance is an explanation of the use of each item. Item definitions may include:

- Item tag or label and full name.
- Table in which it is found.
- Position in table (word number and bit position/level number).
- Item use; e.g., table control item, entry structure key item, string control item, data item.
- Purpose of the item.

- Item coding, depending upon the item type. For example:
    - Symbolic - character code used.
    - Integer - binary or binary coded decimal.
    - Fraction - scaling factor.
    - Mixed number, fixed point - point position.
    - Status - the maximum number of conditions, form of status values (symbolic or numeric binary), a list of all acceptable status values or conditions.
- Accessibility factor - coded to indicate machine instruction modifiers that can expedite retrieving and storing of the item; e.g., FW (full word), LHW or RHW (left- or right-hand word), B (byte size), M (mask necessary).

SECTION 4. PROGRAM ASSEMBLING, LOADING, AND MAINTENANCE PROCEDURES

Section 4 of the manual shall provide information on the specific procedures necessary for the programmer to maintain the programs that make up the system.

4.1 Input/Output Requirements

Included in this paragraph shall be the requirements concerning the equipment and materials needed to support the necessary maintenance tasks. Materials may, for example, include card decks for loading a maintenance program and the inputs which represent the changes to be made. When a support system is being used, this paragraph should reference the appropriate manual.

4.2 Procedures

The procedures, presented in a step-by-step manner, shall detail the method of preparing the inputs, such as the keypunching, structuring, and sequencing of inputs. The operations or steps to be followed in setting up, running, and terminating the maintenance task on the equipment shall be given.

4.3 Verification

This paragraph will include those requirements and procedures necessary to check the performance of a program section following its modification.

4.4 Special Maintenance Programs

This paragraph shall contain an inventory and description of any special programs used to maintain the system.

4.5 Other Special Maintenance Procedures

This paragraph shall contain any special procedures required which have not been delineated elsewhere in this section. Specific information that may be appropriate for presentation would include:

- Requirements, procedures, and verification which may be necessary to maintain the system input/output components, such as the data base.
- Requirements, procedures, and verification methods necessary to perform a Library Maintenance System run.

4.6 Error Conditions

A description of error conditions, not previously documented, may also be included. This description shall include an explanation of the source of the error and recommended methods to correct it.

4.7 Listings

Under separate cover as an appendix to this document will be listings of coding statements in symbolic programming language or higher level language with machine language listings, if required. Annotations shall be provided to introduce components of the system. Clarifying remarks and comments appropriate to particular instructions shall be made. The listing annotations will be in accord with system flowcharts.

EVALUATION REPORT

The Evaluation Report (see Illustration 7-3) shows a comparison between the operational system and the system design specifications and criteria. The functions and capabilities of the live system are evaluated relative to the requirements stated in the Functional Description and System Design Report. The purpose of this report is to demonstrate whether the live system has met design specifications.

Too few organizations periodically evaluate systems once they become operational. Evaluation should include looking at components of a system to see whether they bear a consistent relationship to each other and to the system design objectives. With modular systems, one can evaluate a module before proceeding to the next phase of full system implementation. Installing major systems on a modular basis gives better management control of the project and simplifies identifying the parts of the system that must be modified or updated to reflect the environmental dynamics of a business organization. Each module evolving from the conceptual stage to the development stage can be tailored to new organizational needs that have emerged. This means that integration and evaluation will take place in phases or steps and that the cost of incremental implementation can be directly related to each subsystem.

The Evaluation Report summarizes the history of the project and cites relevant documents and reports. The major performance requirements or goals of the system are described. The capabilities of the operational system are then compared with the stated performance requirements. For example, the response time of the operational system may be evaluated relative to the response time specified in the design documents. The system evaluation procedure should compare the stated objectives of the system (better service, cost avoidance, improved reporting) with the system's actual performance.

The post-installation evaluation should have the following goals:

- The actual performance of the system should be compared with the planned performance.

- The objectives actually being met by the system should be compared with the planned objectives.

- A final comparison should be made between actual resources required to develop the system and estimated resources.

- Potentials to improve the operational system should be defined and documented for further consideration.

- A letter for delivery to the user should indicate that all work on the project has been completed. A copy of this letter should be signed by the user and be placed in the Project Folder.

EVALUATION REPORT

TABLE OF CONTENTS

ILLUSTRATION 7-3.

SECTION 1. GENERAL

1.1 Purpose of Evaluation Report

The purpose of the Evaluation Report should be described in the following words, modified as appropriate:

> This Evaluation Report for (Project Name) (Project Number) is written to:
>
> - Determine if the operational system has met design specifications.
> - Identify unplanned system limitations.

1.2 Project References

A brief summary of the references applicable to the history and development of the project should be provided. A list of applicable documents shall be included. At least the following shall be specified by author or source, reference number and titles:

- User Request
- Functional Description
- System Design Report
- Test Plan
- Operations Manual

SECTION 2. SYSTEM SUMMARY

This section shall provide a general description written in non-ADP language of the computer application.

2.1 Background

Any information concerning the background or the uses and purposes of the system that serves to orient the reader should be included. Reference should be made to relevant higher order and parallel systems. The relationships between this project and other capabilities being developed concurrently should be described.

2.2 Objectives

Statements of the major performance requirements or goals of the system should be included. These statements should be concise and may include examples.

SECTION 3. DETAILED ANALYSIS

3.1 Specific Performance Requirements

This paragraph shall compare performance characteristics of the operational system to system specifications contained in the Functional Description and System Design Report.

3.1.1 Accuracy and Validity

This paragraph shall discuss whether the system satisfies accuracy requirements. The following items must be considered:

- Accuracy requirements of mathematical calculations.
- Logical and legal accuracy of alphanumeric data.
- Accuracy of transmitted data.

3.1.2 Timing

This paragraph shall discuss whether the live system satisfies timing requirements. The following timing requirements shall be considered:

- Throughput time.
- Response time to queries and to updates of data files.
- Response time of major functions.
- Sequential relationship of functions.
- Priorities imposed by types of inputs and changes in modes of operation.
- Timing requirements for the range of traffic load under varying operating conditions.

3.2 System Functions

This paragraph shall discuss the individual functions performed by the live system, and compare them to design specifications.

3.3 Inputs/Outputs

This paragraph shall discuss live system inputs and outputs and compare them to system specifications.

3.4 Data Characteristics

This paragraph shall compare the storage of the data elements used by the application to design specifications.

3.5 Failure Contingencies

This paragraph shall discuss live failures relative to design specifications.

BIBLIOGRAPHY

James L. Adams. **Conceptual Blockbusting: A Guide to Better Ideas.** W. H. Freeman & Company, San Francisco, 1974.

Suad Alagic and Michael A. Arbib. **The Design of Well-Structured and Correct Programs.** Springer-Verlab, New York, 1978.

Leon K. Albrecht. **Organization and Management of Information Processing Systems.** The Macmillan Company, New York, 1973.

Robert N. Anthony. **Planning and Control Systems: A Framework for Analysis.** Graduate School of Business Administration, Harvard University, Cambridge, Massachusetts, 1965.

M. I. Bernstein. "Hardware is Easy: It's Software That's Hard." **Datamation,** November 15, 1978, pp. 32, 34, 36.

Marilyn Bohl. **Flowcharting Techniques.** Science Research Associates, Inc., Chicago, 1971.

Marilyn Bohl. **Tools for Structured Design.** Science Research Associates, Inc., Chicago, 1978.

Marilyn Bohl. **A Guide for Programmers.** Prentice-Hall, Inc., Englewood Cliffs, New Jersey, 1978.

Dick H. Brandon. **Management Standards for Data Processing.** Van Nostrand Reinhold Company, New York, 1963.

Frederick P. Brooks, Jr. **The Mythical Man-Month: Essays on Software Engineering.** Addison-Wesley Publishing Company, Reading, Massachusetts, 1975.

John G. Burch, Jr. and Felix R. Strater, Jr. **Information Systems: Theory and Practice.** Hamilton Publishing Company, Santa Barbara, California, 1974.

Ned Chapin. **Flowcharts.** Auerbach Publishers, Princeton, New Jersey, 1971.

Daniel J. Cougar and Robert W. Knapp. **Systems Analysis Techniques.** John Wiley & Sons, New York, 1974.

William H. Desmonde. **Real-Time Data Processing Systems: Introductory Concepts.** Prentice-Hall, Inc., Englewood Cliffs, New Jersey, 1964.

Norman L. Enger. **Putting MIS to Work: Managing the Management Information System.** American Management Association, New York, 1969.

Norman L. Enger. **Management Standards for Developing Information Systems.** American Management Association, New York, 1976.

Thomas R. Gildersleeve. "Writing Legible Code." **Datamation,** February 1979, pp. 191-193.

George A. Gleim. **Program Flowcharting.** Holt, Rinehart & Winston, Inc., New York, 1970.

Max Gray and Keith London. **Documentation Standards.** Brandon/Systems Press, Inc., Princeton, New Jersey, 1969.

William L. Harper. **Data Processing Documentation: Standards, Procedures and Applications.** Prentice-Hall, Inc., Englewood Cliffs, New Jersey, 1973.

Robert V. Head. **Real-Time Business Systems.** Holt, Rinehart & Winston, Inc., New York, 1964.

Edward O. Joslin and Richard A. Bassler. **Managing Data Processing.** College Readings, Inc., Clifton, Virginia, 1976.

Edward O. Joslin. **Computer Selection.** Augmented Edition. The Technology Press, Inc., Fairfax Station, Virginia, 1977.

Harry Katzan, Jr. **Systems Design and Documentation: An Introduction to the HIPO Method.** Van Nostrand Reinhold Company, New York, 1976.

Walter J. Kennevan and Edward O. Joslin. **Management and Computer Systems.** College Readings, Inc., Clifton, Virginia, 1973.

Brian W. Kernighan and P. J. Plauger. **The Elements of Programming Style.** Second Edition. McGraw-Hill Book Company, New York, 1978.

Philip Kraft. **Programmers and Managers.** Springer-Verlag, New York, 1977.

Leonard J. Krauss. **Administering and Controlling the Company Data Processing Function.** Prentice-Hall, Inc., Englewood Cliffs, New Jersey, 1969.

Robert S. Kuehne, Herbert W. Lindberg, and William F. Baron. **Manual of Computer Documentation Standards with Forms.** Prentice-Hall, Inc., Englewood Cliffs, New Jersey, 1972.

Clement A. Lamb. "DP and the User: A Matter of Planning." **Datamation**, November 1, 1978, pp. 169, 170, 177.

K. G. Lockyer. **An Analysis to Critical Path Analysis.** Pitman Publishing Corporation, New York, 1964.

Keith R. London. **Documentation Standards.** Second Edition. Petrocelli Books, New York, 1974.

James Martin. **Design of Real-Time Computer Systems.** Prentice-Hall, Inc., Englewood Cliffs, New Jersey, 1967.

L. Daniel Massey and John Heptonstall. **EDP Feasibility Analysis.** D. H. Mark Publishing Company, Braintree, Massachusetts, 1968.

Adrian M. McDonough. **Information Economics and Management Systems.** McGraw-Hill Book Company, New York, 1963.

Philip W. Metzger. **Managing a Programming Project.** Prentice-Hall, Inc., Englewood Cliffs, New Jersey, 1973.

Edwin Newman. **Strictly Speaking.** Warner Books, New York, 1974.

Stanford L. Optner. **Systems Analysis for Business Management.** Prentice-Hall, Inc., Englewood Cliffs, New Jersey, 1960.

Henry H. Petersohn. **Computer Failure and Energy Shortages.** The Technology Press, Inc., Fairfax Station, Virginia, 1979.

John P. Robinson and James D. Graviss. **Documentation Standards Manual for Computer Systems.** Association for Systems Management, Cleveland, Ohio, 1973.

Gary B. Shelly and Thomas J. Cashman. **Introduction of Flowcharting and Computer Programming Logic.** Anaheim Publishing Company, Fullerton, California, 1972.

U. S. Department of Defense. **Automated Data System Documentation Standards Manual,** 4120.17-M. Government Printing Office, Washington, D.C., December 1972.

U. S. Department of the Navy. **Automated Data System Documentation Standards.** SECNAVINST 5233.1A. Government Printing Office, Washington, D.C., June 1973.

Michael G. Walker. "A Theory for Software Reliability." **Datamation,** September 1978, pp. 211, 212, 214.

George W. Weinwurm. **On the Management of Computer Programming.** Auerbach Publishers, Inc., Princeton, New Jersey, 1970.

Leon A. Youssef. **Systems Analysis and Design.** Reston Publishing Company, Inc., Reston, Virginia, 1975.

INDEX